NIGHTMARRIAGE

NIGHTMARRIAGE

eLectio Publishing
Little Elm, TX

www.eLectioPublishing.com

Copyright © 2013 Chad Thomas Johnston

All rights reserved.

Cover copyright 2013 by Chad Thomas Johnston

Cover design by Chad Thomas Johnston

ISBN: 0615825559

ISBN-13: 978-0615825557

Scripture quotations marked (ESV) are from The Holy Bible, English Standard Version® (ESV®), copyright © 2001 by Crossway, a publishing ministry of Good News Publishers. Used by permission. All rights reserved.

Scripture quotations marked (NIV) are taken from the Holy Bible, New International Version®, NIV®. Copyright © 1973, 1978, 1984, 2011 by Biblica, Inc.™ Used by permission of Zondervan. All rights reserved worldwide. www.zondervan.com The "NIV" and "New International Version" are trademarks registered in the United States Patent and Trademark Office by Biblica, Inc.™

Scripture quotations marked (KJV) are taken from The Authorized (King James) Version. Rights in the Authorized Version in the United Kingdom are vested in the Crown. Reproduced by permission of the Crown's patentee, Cambridge University Press.

Unless otherwise noted, scripture quotations are taken from the New King James Version®. Copyright © 1982 by Thomas Nelson, Inc. Used by permission. All rights reserved.

Dedication

For the lovely ladies in my life, Becki and Evie.

NIGHTMARRIAGE Credits

Edited by Jennifer Harris Dault. For inquiries regarding Jennifer's editing services, direct correspondence to her email address: doveintheattic@gmail.com. In addition to her work on *Nightmarriage*, Jennifer also spearheaded, edited, and contributed writing to a book titled *The Modern Magnificat: Women Responding to the Call of God*, published by Nurturing Faith, Inc. in 2012. Purchase it at http://nurturingfaith.info.

Additional editing on "Abra-Chad-abra!: Marital Magic," "My Wife, the Black Hole," and "Honeymoonwalking (to Jail)" by Cathy Warner. As owner and host of Bainbridge Island Ink, Cathy offers a retreat on Puget Sound for writers, as well as writing services, editing, and workshops. Read more about it at http://www.cathywarner.com/.

Mixed media cover art by Chad Thomas Johnston. Special thanks to Brandon and Joanna Gillette and Meredith Holladay for contributing cutlery to the photo shoot. Additional thanks to my brother-in-law, Matt Damon, for teaching me how to layer images in GIMP (The GNU Image Manipulation Program) to achieve the desired results.

Interior art by BARRR (Jason Barr), Dan Billen, Ben Chlapek, Megan Frauenhoffer, Danny Joe Gibson, Mark Montgomery, and Darin M. White. Artist information appears in Appendix E.

Table of Contents

Nightmarriage, Social Media, and You, the Reader	1
Wedding Photo of Chad and Becki by Caleb Schickedanz	2
Author's Foreword: Tying the Knot at Two O'clock in the Morning	3
Art: "We Found Each Other in the Psychic Other of God's Love," Watercolor by BARRR	7
Abra-Chad-abra!: Marital Magic	9
Art: "My Wife, the Black Hole (Panel A)," Mixed Media Art by Danny Joe Gibson	22
Art: "My Wife, the Black Hole (Panel B)," Mixed Media Art by Danny Joe Gibson	23
My Wife, the Black Hole	25
Art: "Shoes for My Wife, Secret Centipede," Digital Art by Mark Montgomery	34
Putting the "Die" in Diarrhea	35
Art: "Wedlockness," Ink Illustration by Ben Chlapek	39
The Art of the Pity Party, Perfected	41
Art: "Hearts and Jumper Cables," Mixed Media Art by Danny Joe Gibson	46
Hearts and Jumper Cables	47
Art: "Transmission Impossible," Mixed Media Art by Danny Joe Gibson	54
Dew Ewe Here Watt Eye Hear?	55
Art: "There Will Be Consequences," Ink Illustration by Megan Frauenhoffer	61
	63

Knives and Wives

    Art: "Michael Jackson, King of Pop (Not to Be Confused with 'King of Soda')," Watercolor by **BARRR**   65

    Art: "Gary Coleman in Cowboy Hat," Watercolor by **BARRR**   66

Honeymoonwalking (to Jail)   67

    Art: "Clarence Clemons, Saxophone King," Watercolor by **BARRR**   84

    Art: "Rodney King, King of Rodney," Watercolor by **BARRR**   85

When Pads with Wings Fly   87

Pass Me a Scissors, Please   89

    Art: "With This Cloaking Devise (sic) I Thee Wed," Ink Illustration by **BARRR**   92

With This Cloaking Device, I Thee Wed   93

    Sonogram Photo of Evangeline Sofia Johnston   100

Blessed Are the Tentmakers   101

    Art: "Blessed Are the Tentmakers," Watercolor by Darin M. White   105

The Scatological Opportunist   107

    Art: "Rainbow Trout Topped with Rainbow Sherbet," Colored Pencil Illustration by Darin M. White   111

Rainbow Trout Topped with Rainbow Sherbet   113

    Art: "Pregnancy Brain: Memory-Bank Robber," Digital Art by Mark Montgomery   118

Pregnancy Brain: Memory-Bank Robber   119

Our Hearts Are Open, but Our Doors Are Locked   125

    Art: "Umbilical Floor Lamp" Mixed Media Art by Danny Joe Gibson   132

The Paralytic Shopping Spree	133
Art: "Baby Promises to Never Flood the World with Tears," Mixed Media Art by Danny Joe Gibson	139
County Road Something-or-Other	141
Art: "The Keys to Her Heart," Digital Art by Dan Billen	147
The Heart, a Home under Construction	149
Photo of Evie by Becki's Twin, Katie Damon	153
Art: "The Diaper Filled with Gold at the End of the Baby-Rainbow," Crayola by Baby Evie	154
Acknowledgments	155

Supplemental Materials: Emphasis on the "Mental"

Appendix A: 140 Character Chronicles: #Marriage, #Parenthood, & #More via Twitter	161
Appendix B: Feline Groovy	175
Exhibit 1: Homemade First Anniversary Card for Becki	175
Exhibit 2: Cat Blanket for Baby Evie by Christy Fiola Miller	177
Appendix C: "Everybody's Talking but Me (I'm Yelling)": Free Virtual Vinyl MP3 Narrated by CTJ	179
Appendix D: Recipes	181
Evil: A Chili Recipe by CTJ	181
Boom Boom Legumes: A Cowboy Bean Recipe by CTJ	183
Chili con Carnage: A Chili Recipe by Ax-Wielder Brandon S. Gillette	184
Appendix E: Author and Artist Information	185
About Author Chad Thomas Johnston, Author Photo by Danny Joe Gibson	185
About Artist Jason Barr	189
About Artist Dan Billen	191
About Artist Ben Chlapek	193
About Artist Megan Frauenhoffer	195
About Artist Danny Joe Gibson	197
About Artist Mark A. Montgomery	201
About Artist Darin M. White	203

Nightmarriage, Social Media, and You, the Reader

If you enjoy *Nightmarriage* and want to help eLectio Publishing promote it, consider yourself a member of our public relations team!

1) If you use Pinterest, visit *Nightmarriage*'s Pinterest page (http://pinterest.com/saintupid/nightmarriage/) and repin the book art on your boards. All images will direct traffic to a page on Chad Thomas Johnston's website featuring published excerpts, purchasing information, and more.
2) If you use Twitter, tell your followers about the book. Be sure to include the hashtag #Nightmarriage in the tweet.
3) Tell your Facebook friends about it, too.

Chad Thomas Johnston and eLectio Publishing thank you for your support!

Wedding Photo of Chad and Becki by Caleb Schickedanz.

(Note: Color versions of images appearing in this book are available at http://pinterest.com/saintupid/nightmarriage.)

Author's Foreword: Tying the Knot at Two O'clock in the Morning

★ ★ ★

When I first told my friend, singer-songwriter Sam Billen, that I was writing a memoir titled *Nightmarriage*, he said, "But it's not about *your* marriage, right?"[1]

"Well, it's not something that's going to land me in the marital doghouse, if that's what you mean," I replied. He responded with nervous laughter, as if he had no idea how to reconcile the title of the book with anything other than a nightmarish vision of marriage.

When I showed him the cover art, the blood drained from his face like water from a bathtub.

"But dude, there are, like, axes and knives on the cover," he said. "Has your wife seen this?"

"She helped me arrange the knives for the photo shoot, actually," I said. "The book's about my marriage, but it's humorous in tone—heartwarming, too, I think. It's not like I'm airing our dirty laundry in public."

Of course, the public can probably see and smell our dirty laundry without any help from us. Even now, the mountain of dirty cloth diapers at our house dwarfs mighty Mount Oread here in Lawrence, Kansas.

---

[1] The audiobook version of *Nightmarriage* features music from Sam's latest album, *Places*. Many fine Interweb retailers carry this record, including Amazon, iTunes, and Bandcamp.

"The title may sound scary, but it's just wordplay," I continued. "It's a portmanteau of the words 'nightmare' and 'marriage.'"

"A portmanteau . . ." he said, the color returning to his freckled face. "I get it, man. A light just came on in my brain."[2]

Sam teaches English as a Second Language (ESL) at the University of Kansas, so I assumed his students asked questions about things like idioms, portmanteaus, and slang on a regular basis. Apparently, I assumed correctly.

Around the same time, eLectio Publishing CEO Jesse S. Greever informed me of the company's plans to distribute *Nightmarriage* internationally in over eighty e-book formats. Upon hearing this, I immediately thought of another person who had been perplexed by the title of this collection.

My mother teaches an ESL course at the church my father pastors, so she often interacts with international students, including some who are not enrolled in her class. When she shared the title of the book with one such Iranian college student named Hadi, he said, "You mean people get married at night in America, Holly?"

I write about Sam and Hadi because I wish to clarify a few things about the nature of *Nightmarriage* before encouraging readers to wade hip-deep into our marital and parental follies. While the title of the book may suggest I am offering the reader a delicious dish of marital discord served with a side of psychosis, *Nightmarriage* is anything but a seedy read. It has nothing to do with tying the knot at 2:00 a.m. either.

---

[2] In December of 2011, Sam collaborated with my brother-in-law Matt to create alightgoeson.org—a website that features Christmas songs by Sam, his brother Dan, Japan's The Tenniscoats, Halfhanded Cloud, and many more. Each song on the site corresponds with a work of art or video. Dan Billen and Danny Joe Gibson, who created art for *Nightmarriage*, both contributed to the compilation. Sam's featured song, "A Light Goes On," also appears on his album, *Places*. I provided a work of art and a song ("Away in a Manger of Dreams") for the collection, too. Visit http://alightgoeson.org/ and download the music for free.

Nightmarriage is a whimsical memoir that explores the terrors of marriage and the perils of parenthood. I wrote it not as a seasoned husband or father, but as one who still has much to learn. In both of these roles, I remain as awkward as a boy learning to ride a bicycle; I wobble, teeter this way and that, and crash into mailboxes and parked cars occasionally.

Early versions of the essays that appear in the book first surfaced at chadthomasjohnston.com between 2010 and 2012. I decided to rework my blog entries because I undercooked the original writings in some places and burnt them in others. In the end, I can only hope these essays feel uniformly warm, and not hot on the outside and cold in the middle like a frozen burrito after a few rotations in a convenience-store microwave.

Regarding my approach to writing about my marriage, I once witnessed a minor celebrity comedian (who shall remain nameless here) dehumanize his wife for the duration of his drunken set at a club in Cleveland, Ohio. By the end of the night, he had transformed her into a living punch line—something I want to avoid at all costs in this book. That being said, I hope *Nightmarriage* reads as a loving lampoon, and not as a heartless harpoon aimed at my wife.

Regarding the scatological slant of some of the stories in *Nightmarriage*, I fear I am something of an eighth grader trapped in the body of a thirty-four-year-old man. As a minister's son, I cannot help but think I confused my father's study of eschatology with scatology at an early age, and cultivated an interest in the subject to become more like him.

Fortunately, Jesse S. Greever is likewise an eternal eighth grader. When we initially discussed the publication of *Nightmarriage*, he was crestfallen that he could not offer a scratch-and-sniff edition of the book for the benefit of essays like "Putting the 'Die' in Diarrhea" and "The Scatological Opportunist."

In order to ease Jesse's suffering, I have provided sensory experiences for the reader in other ways. To supply sufficient visual stimulation, for example, I asked seven artists I know to contribute original works to the book. Readers who remain kindergartners at heart, preferring books with pictures to those that have none, will find *Nightmarriage* a rewarding read. Should those same readers wish to find out more about the artists whose works appear in these pages, Appendix E features contact information, website addresses, and more.

As for the other senses, Appendix D consists entirely of recipes designed to nip at readers' nostrils and tantalize taste buds. Where hearing is concerned, I have provided links to free albums (like the one mentioned in footnote two) for the reader to download and enjoy.[3] With regard to the tactile dimension, I can only hope this book touches the hearts of those who read it.

Finally, to you who follow me on Twitter, Facebook, Instagram, Pinterest, *IMAGE Journal*'s "Good Letters" blog, or chadthomasjohnston.com, thank you for shelling out your schillings for this book that Jesse and I have been shilling so shamelessly. My wife Becki, our one-year-old Evie, and our five felines also thank you.

May all your domestic dreams come true, and all your marital nightmares give way to laughter, portmanteaus, and publishing contracts.

—Chad Thomas Johnston, May 2013

---

[3] Production of an audiobook version of *Nightmarriage* will begin after the release of the print edition. Check http://chadthomasjohnston.com for details. The narrator is Brandon S. Gillette, whose ax appears on the cover of this book and in the essay, "Our Hearts Are Open, but Our Doors Are Locked."

"We Found Each Other in the Psychic Other of God's Love," watercolor by BARRR.

Abra-Chad-abra!: Marital Magic

★ ★ ★

The Woman Who Willed a River into Being

Like God, who dispelled darkness with the words, "Let there be light," my wife Becki issues a command and the universe obeys—at least to some extent. With her powers, she once willed a river into being, and I suppose that was as good a reason as any to marry her.

It happened in June of 2007.

Becki and I had been in a long-distance relationship for five months. With our cell phones at our ears for hours at a time, we irradiated our brains in the name of love. When we tired of talking on the phone, we traveled the six hundred miles separating Lawrence, Kansas, from Milwaukee, Wisconsin, to see each other in person.

When Becki flew to Lawrence to visit me that June, we walked down historic Massachusetts Street, otherwise known as "Mass" to the city's residents. Shortly after we made our way onto Sixth Street, Becki looked across the road and saw the entrance to a bridge.

"Is there a river over there?" she asked.

"No," I replied. "I think it's just an overpass."

I moved from Springfield, Missouri, to Lawrence in August of 2006 to pursue a PhD in film studies. Having lived in the city for ten months, it seemed absurd to me that Becki, who had only been there a few days, would think she could possibly know something about Lawrence that I did not.

A month after moving to Kansas, I crossed that bridge on my way to the DMV. I would have welcomed the radiance of a river en route to that place, where waiting lines rival the length of the muddy Mississippi and people drown in paperwork. As far as I could remember, however, I saw no such thing.

"No, I think there's a river over there," she said.

She insisted we pay the bridge a visit, and I knew better than to resist. Attempting to bend Becki's will is a challenge on par with redirecting the course of a river, real or imagined.

As we walked along the bridge, whispers of white noise swelled to roaring television snow. We looked over the railing and saw the larger-than-life, liquid equivalent of a Kansas copperhead flowing below us, its ripples shining metallic like scales in the sun.

"I *knew* there was a river here," Becki said.

"I didn't," I said, my cheeks burning with embarrassment.

While cartographers and historians would contend that the Kansas River, otherwise known as the Kaw, existed before Becki visited me, I prefer to think it sprang from her brain that day. I imagine her uttering the words, "Let there be a river," and I picture the Kaw carving its way across eastern Kansas then and there—scrawling its signature on the land with a flowing fountain pen. It coursed its way into our hearts that day, too, supplying us both with life like a shared artery.

We returned to the river several times that week. One day, we even picnicked on the concrete embankment overlooking the dam's spillway. We ate sandwiches and apple chips, and uncorked a bottle of Hogue Riesling in honor of the Kaw—the river that belonged to us.

It has been ours ever since.

* * *

Living in a Snow Globe

Becki and I met because I recorded a Christmas album, of all things. Unlike Becki, I could not will one into being simply by proclaiming, "Let there be a Christmas album!"

I used my own superpower—Obsessive-Compulsive Disorder (OCD)—to complete this labor of Yuletide love. With the exception of a glockenspiel part here and some background vocals there, I arranged, performed, and recorded all the album's vocal and instrumental parts myself.

That being said, I suppose I met Becki because of my OCD.

After four years of living with an anxiety that had no name, my therapist—a kindhearted Catholic counselor named Troy—diagnosed me with the disorder in August of 2004. While I already knew I had bats in my belfry, I took comfort in the knowledge that the species inhabiting my brain responded favorably to therapy and medication. I continued to see "Counselor Troy," as I referred to him in homage to *Star Trek: The Next Generation*, through 2006.

A few weeks after my diagnosis, my friends Matt and Rebecca gave me a copy of a Christmas album they created as husband and wife. Their homespun holiday record compelled me to create my own. To this day, I cannot say why—people with OCD cannot always make heads or tails of their obsessions. I only know that I, too, wanted to sing about Christmas trees and sleigh bells and baby Jesus, with his nose so bright.

As I gained some mastery over my disorder, I realized that if I occupy my mind with a creative project, I leave less room for fears to flourish like weeds in a garden and choke out my peace.

In other words, better a cheery Christmas album the whole world can hear than the sounds of scarier obsessions spinning and skipping in my head like broken records only I can hear.

Recording a Christmas album is a bizarre business, as it is not something one does over a gravy-and-giblet-fueled Thanksgiving holiday bender. Musicians make Christmas records months before cartons of eggnog appear in grocery store refrigerators.

My Christmas season began in October in 2004. I lived in Springfield, Missouri, at the time and shared a house with two friends who also wrote and recorded music. By day, I taught Introduction to Public Speaking in the Department of Communication at Missouri State University. By night, I recorded my Christmas album, *All is Calm, All is Bright*, in my basement—a workspace with a mold problem and a ceiling height of six feet.[5]

For the next month and a half, I labored on my magnum opus of mirth and myrrh. During this time, my parents, who lived two hours away from me in Rolla, Missouri, began to express concern about my increasing isolation when we spoke on the phone.

I had been single most of my twenty-six years, thanks in part to my delightful disorder. Mom and Dad, knowing how much I longed for a wife, said I would never find a spouse if I continued to spend my spare time alone in that damp dungeon of a basement, recording Christmas songs only a few people would ever hear.

I did feel like I had been living in a snow globe. I had become a hermit in a hermetically sealed holiday world, and I knew it. All the

---

[4] Download the album for free at https://soundcloud.com/saint_upid/sets/all-is-calm-all-is-bright.

[5] One thing I learned immediately: Mold, though green, is not a suitable substitute for decorative garland.

same, I told my parents I was in therapy, on medication, and channeling my obsessive tendencies into a creative project that celebrated the birth of our Lord and Savior. They continued to insist that I needed to leave my basement more often if I wanted to meet a mate.

I was frankly a little surprised when it turned out they were wrong.

After selling the completed Christmas album locally in December, I returned to my basement in June of 2005 to remix and remaster the album for a rerelease the following holiday season. After two months, I decided I had labored too long on the record not to offer it online to the MP3-downloading public.

The new version of the album featured three new recordings—an atmospheric instrumental titled "Away in a Manger of Dreams," the catatonic but cranky "Frosty the Psycho Shoegazer Snowman," and a Jesus-and-Mary-Chain-inspired scorcher capable of liquefying Frosty in seconds, titled "Holiday Trash Medley."

I released this version of the record on PureVolume.com as a free download in November of 2005.[6] Two weeks later, I received a Facebook message from a Wisconsin native named Becki.

The message consisted of all lowercase letters and read, "are you the chad johnston who's on purevolume and has absolutely amazing music? i figured there aren't too many people with your name, but who knows? :)"

She explained that her twin, Katie, had discovered my music and shared it with her. I could hardly believe that women who lived in

---

[6] In 2011, I reissued my Christmas album again with three additional songs ("Silver Bells of Destruction," "This is What Child this Is," and "Bethlehem [The 51st State]"), and gave the collection a new name: *Stalking Stuffers: Coal for the Stocking in Your Soul*. Download this version of the album for free at http://noisetrade.com/stalkingstuffers.

Wisconsin—twins, no less—had discovered my music and searched for me on the Internet. I replied, thanking Becki for her interest in my work, and soon began exchanging Facebook messages with her with some regularity.

"I have fans in Wisconsin," I told my coworker Bryan, who taught the same coursework I did. "And not just any fans, dude. *Twin sisters.*"

"Ooh, way to go, Chaddeus!" Bryan said. "Twins!"

This idea seemed especially exotic to both of us—as it probably has to men for time immemorial, I suppose. Granted, few men who meet twin sisters ever find themselves in romantic entanglements with both women at the same time, but that hardly mattered to Bryan or me.

Despite all the excitement, I never expected my exchange with Becki to amount to anything more than a casual correspondence. She and Katie lived too far away for me to consider the possibility that I would know either of them in anything other than a superficial way.

Katie eventually wrote me, too. Over the following months, she and Becki sent me more messages—the only fan mail I ever received as a musician, really.

* * *

Milwaukee Talkie

If the twins regarded me as a rock star, however, they obviously did not see me as the sort that inspired fits or fainting. When Becki and I started talking on the phone three months after we began corresponding on Facebook, she ended our conversations almost as soon as they began with the words, "I have to go, Chad."[7] Katie did the same when I spoke with her.

I know now that, at the time, the twins were betrothed to their textbooks—their hearts promised to their professions. Both of them were enrolled in degree programs to become physician assistants, and if they talked to me too long, they felt like they were being unfaithful to their studies.

Becki and I first talked on the phone after she sent me a message saying she needed "dating advice from a Christian brother." I love to help people, and I felt honored that she would trust me with the details of her dating life, so I agreed to call her.

After the first and only phone call we would have for a while, she told me via email that she had been unable to salvage her relationship. While both of us obviously benefitted from this breakup in the long run, neither of us foresaw our future together at that point.

We began to talk on the phone with greater frequency after I moved to Lawrence six months later. Around the same time, Becki temporarily relocated to the tiny town of Tomah, Wisconsin, to complete a clinical rotation for her degree. Neither of us knew anyone in our new towns, so we reached out to each other in our loneliness. Our conversations began to last a little longer, but Becki still ended them without warning with the words, "I have to go, Chad."

That year for Halloween, I dressed as a sleep-deprived graduate student with bed head and bloodshot eyes, and I celebrated with my two cats, Charlotte and Sophie, and my textbooks. Becki, on the other hand, donned a fetching bumblebee costume and black

---

[7] Becki and Katie both have Wisconsin accents. In their mouths, the letter "o" elongates as if it is made of elastic. The word "hose" becomes "h-o-o-o-se." "I have to go" becomes "I have to g-o-o-o."

stockings for a party at a friend's apartment. When I saw pictures of her in that outfit on Facebook, I wanted that bee to call me "Honey."

I began babbling to my friends at church and in my department at school about this woman who lived in Wisconsin. They looked at me as if to say, "Everyone knows long-distance relationships are doomed to end up in the dating dustbin. Savor Lawrence's bumper crop of college babes and forget about Wisconsin." This, of course, came from beer-swilling, cheese-eating sages—seasoned supporters of Wisconsin's primary exports—who also happened to be single.

While I had attempted to date a few women in Lawrence, they lacked Becki's intelligence and warmth, her faith in God, her goodness, her sweetness, and her love for movies and music.[8] Most of all though, none of them were bumblebees in black stockings.

One day, after I shared several war stories from the dating battlefield with Becki on the phone, she said, "Chad, after you're done with your PhD program, I'll marry you if you want—I mean, if you're still single." Of course, as soon as she made this proclamation, she had to go.

No one had ever said anything like that to me before. Even though we had not yet met in person, the idea of marrying her appealed to me.

With my headphones on, I went for a walk that day, following the red brick sidewalks in my neighborhood while listening to Imogen Heap's song "Say Goodnight and Go" over and over. It reminded me of the woman from Wisconsin who could not bid me goodnight without saying "I have to go" first.

---

[8] It occurs to me that the warmth I sensed coming from Becki might have been cell phone radiation.

Shortly after Christmas that year, I drove ten hours to meet Becki even though I was only able to stay in Milwaukee for thirty-six hours because of her work schedule. The bats in my belfry had a field day while I was in Wisconsin.

Sleep-deprived because of anxiety about the trip, fatigued from travel, and unfamiliar with my surroundings in Milwaukee, I found myself especially vulnerable to my OCD during my stay with Becki and Katie. Mostly, the blind mammals in my mind flapped their webbed wings as I thought about what might or might not be possible with Becki.

Following my brain's lead, my body—and most especially, my stomach—flooded with fear. This left no room for food, which meant I ate fewer than two bites in Becki's company. She would later tell me this led her to believe I might have an eating disorder of some sort.

By the end of my only full day with her, however, her warmth began to cut through the craziness in my brain like sunlight breaking through cloud cover. Although she cannot sing to save her life, in a moment I will never forget, she sang along with her favorite Smoking Popes album, *Born to Quit,* as if she might have been trying to save mine.

We entered into a long-distance relationship within a week of my return to Lawrence. In the end, we survived as a couple with all of that space separating us because of Becki's dogged determination. Anytime my anxieties threatened to sabotage us, she persisted in proclaiming her love until the noise in my head quieted down.

Four months after we began dating, Becki earned her Master of Physician Studies degree. At the same time, I became a PhD dropout, withdrawing from my degree program after completing one year of coursework. I had become disillusioned with my department—with the unfriendly faculty, with the absence of organization, and most of all, with the lack of funding.

No longer preoccupied with becoming a professor, I decided to pursue my lifelong love of writing in earnest. While I had a day job that paid the bills, I barely had two wooden nickels to rub together. Still, I never considered myself poor because writing enriched my life. Becki stayed with me through all of this despite my downward mobility and delusions of literary grandeur.

Five months after I became a PhD dropout, and nine months after we began dating at a distance, Becki told me she wanted to move to Lawrence. This both touched and terrified me.

On one hand, I could not believe Becki would willingly leave her family—especially her twin—for me. On the other hand, I had not promised her anything permanent at that point, so I worried she would move to Lawrence only for our relationship to fall apart. Ultimately, however, my excitement eclipsed my fears, and I could not wait for Becki to become a Kansan.

The week she told me she wanted to move to Kansas, she interviewed for three physician assistant jobs in the vicinity of Lawrence, and received offers from all three employers within days. Once again, she demonstrated her power to will things into being: "Let there be jobs."

Shortly after accepting the best offer, she willed an apartment in Lawrence to open up. She moved into it with her two cats, Oliver and Othello, in December of 2007. She would adopt a third cat named Omelie later that year, sometime after tiring of her tiny apartment and declaring, "Let there be a house." In June of 2008, she moved into the split tri-level that would become my home, too, when we married in June of 2009.

The only thing she could not will into being was the ring she now wears on her finger. Only I could supply that.

*   *   *

How to Transform a Woman into a Teakettle

Hours after I bought Becki's engagement ring, I invited her to meet me at my apartment for an evening walk to the bridge overlooking our river on an unseasonably warm day in February of 2009. We walked this route often, as the Kaw was a mile away from my place, and we enjoyed walking and talking as we passed Lawrence landmarks along the way.

When we reached the middle of the bridge that night, we reveled in the view. Despite the tepid temperature of the air, the surface of the river remained largely frozen from frostier days. It sparkled in the moonlight like a winding diamond road.

I removed something from my pocket and casually held it aloft for Becki's acknowledgement. In the half-light of the evening, Becki could see the unmistakable shape of a ring between my index finger and thumb, but nothing more.

"And what do we have here?" I said, just before the ring slipped from my fingers, hit the railing of the bridge, and fell into the Kaw.

I looked at Becki in horror, my mouth agape.

"W-w-what was that, Chad?" she stammered. "Was that . . . an engagement ring, Chad?!?"

"I . . . don't . . . know what to say right now," I said, shaking my head in shock. "I . . . I have the box it came in if you want to see that. It's better than nothing, I suppose."

"You have . . . the *box* it came in?" she repeated.

"Yes," I said.

I retrieved a purple, faux-alligator-skin box from my jacket pocket. It reminded me of Becki's purple alligator-skin purse. Every time I saw it I pictured a purple alligator terrifying Florida tourists with its sense of style.

"Look—it's purple. Your favorite color," I said.

"It's purple. My favorite color," she mumbled, too dumbfounded to do anything but repeat my words.

"Oh yeah," I said after a moment's hesitation. "I should probably open it... you know, just in case there's something inside. You never know." I opened the box, revealing a white-gold ring with tiny diamonds set in filigree.

Becki began to squeal like a teakettle on a burner.

"What's going on?! What are you doing?! What's happening?!" she shouted amidst squeals and other noises that might have passed for chipmunk distress calls, had we been in the woods. I bent down on one knee and asked her to marry me.

She said yes, of course.

She continued to squeal. Either she was a teakettle and she was done brewing, or she was a woman who was done with the business of being single.

"I have one question," she said after she calmed down.

"Yes?" I said.

"What on *Earth* did you drop in the river? It looked like a ring to me..."

"Oh, *that*," I said. "That was just a ring from a keychain, Honey. I needed a disposable decoy—something I could 'accidentally' drop into the river."

"I cannot *believe* you did that," she said, laughing.

"Yes, you can," I said.

"You're right," she said. "I can. And I love my ring, by the way. It's beautiful."

Her ring glittered in the moonlight like the winding diamond road below us. Were it not for the ambient light radiating from the city into the sky, the stars might have sparkled in the firmament, too—echoing the ring and the river.

Let there be stars.

"My Wife, the Black Hole (Panel A),"
mixed media by Danny Joe Gibson.

"My Wife, the Black Hole (Panel B),"
mixed media by Danny Joe Gibson.

My Wife, the Black Hole

★ ★ ★

When I first learned Becki could will things into being, I noticed that for each item that materialized at her behest, another disappeared. I initially thought this was simply the price she paid for using her powers—that for each of her actions, there was an equal and opposite reaction.

It seems more probable, however, that things disappear because Becki misplaces them. Her driver's license, her iPad, the power adaptor she uses to charge her phone—all of these have gone missing at one time or another.

As much as I enjoy the taste of my own foot in my mouth, I hesitate to call her absentminded, scatterbrained, or even forgetful—even if the shoe fits. Of course, one can only try a shoe on if one can find it.[9]

In her defense, when it comes to medical matters, she never forgets a thing. I once witnessed her diagnose a patient on a medical drama with something called "trimethylaminuria" long before the doctors on the show reached the same conclusion.

"People with trimethylaminuria have a fishy odor," she explained. "There's an enzyme called . . ."

I heard nothing of the medical explanation that followed because I found her diagnosis semantically ambiguous: Did she mean the

---

[9] Becki has many shoes to lose, too. So many, in fact, that I sometimes think she is secretly a centipede. Only a creature with hundreds of legs needs hundreds of shoes, right?

smell of a fish pulled fresh from a lake, or the smell of the battered, cooked, crispy kind?

Either way, the word "fishy" said it all. I find it fishy, for example, that Becki remembers an eight-syllable word like trimethylaminuria, but forgets where she placed her purse.

With the passage of time, I have developed a hypothesis that may account for Becki's behavior: Maybe—*just maybe*—my wife is a black hole, incarnate.

The objects that vanish into her vortex rarely include those items I wish would disappear. Rubber hair-bands, used Kleenexes, half-empty soda cans, and bobby pins all resist her gravitational pull. For all my efforts to rid our residence of these things, they appear to be as permanent as the pyramids.

Becki's car keys, smartphone, and purse, on the other hand, disappear daily.

"Where are my keys?" she asks me. "I can't find them anywhere."

"Sorry, Hon," I say. "I don't know where they are either."

Of course, when one's wife is a black hole, "*Where* are my keys?" is the wrong question.

I keep quiet, but I want to say, "Don't you mean '*When* are my keys?'"

Stephen Hawking describes a black hole as a "time machine" capable of sending travelers into the near future.[10] If Becki is a black hole then, her possessions probably travel through time as a result of

---

[10] See Hawking's article for *The Daily Mail*, titled "Stephen Hawking: How to Build a Time Machine," at http://www.dailymail.co.uk/home/moslive/article-1269288/STEPHEN-HAWKING-How-build-time-machine.html.

their proximity to her, exiting the present and re-entering the space-time continuum at some unspecified point in the future—usually within a matter of hours or days.[11]

Having seen George Pal's filmic adaptation of H. G. Wells's *The Time Machine*, I know objects that move through time do so without moving in space. When Rod Taylor's character travels into the future in the film, after all, his time machine never moves an inch.

This explains what happened to Becki's debit card shortly after we married. After it disappeared one day, she cancelled it, fearing someone might find it and bankrupt us. Becki found the card a few days later—in her purse, where it belongs.

"I don't understand, Chaddy," she said. "A few days ago, I looked for my debit card in my purse, and it wasn't there. Then I opened it today and—well, it was *there!*" In retrospect, I believe Becki's two-dimensional VISA card traveled through the fourth dimension, leaving the present without ever leaving her three-dimensional purse.[12]

I first suspected there was something different about Becki shortly after she moved from Milwaukee to Lawrence. She called me at

---

[11] Before I even proposed to Becki, our friends Brandon and Joanna bought me a copy of Audrey Niffenegger's best-selling debut, *The Time Traveler's Wife*, for my thirtieth birthday. How prescient of them to present me with a book that would prepare me for a marriage involving time travel!

[12] Upon reading this passage, eLectio Publishing CEO Jesse S. Greever informed me that debit cards are technically three-dimensional objects—they simply happen to be very flat. I did not alter this sentence even though Jesse is, in fact, correct. I told him the reader would understand what I mean.

Also, Jesse despises the phrase "in fact." Any Twitter users reading this book should address a tweet to @JesseSGreever and find a way to include this phrase in the message. Be as creative as possible. Please copy me (@Saint_Upid) on the message, too!

work, panicking because she could not find her car keys. I drove her to work and located her keys after less than fifteen minutes of searching when I returned to her apartment later that day.

I assumed this was an isolated event—a product of her recent move. She was still living out of boxes, after all. One thing troubled me, however: Becki's keys had been in plain sight when I found them. How could she have overlooked them?

I now believe that, sometime before she began searching for them, they blinked out of the present and traveled a few hours into the future. If they had been in the place where I found them when Becki searched for them midday, she would have seen them.

The following week, she lost her Honda Civic. This set off more than a few alarms in my mind. Who was this woman who had moved to Lawrence for me? Would she cause me to disappear someday, too?

It turned out Becki had driven her car to my apartment the night before, and I had given her a ride home in my Dodge Stratus. Both of us forgot she had driven to my place.

Then there is the story of the $396 check.

Well before we married, Becki drove my Stratus to the auto shop for me on one of her days off while I worked. I desperately needed new tires, and she paid for them with her credit card, knowing I would repay her.

That evening, I handed her a check for $396. A few days later, she reminded me that I still needed to pay her for my tires.

"But I already paid you," I said.

"No, you didn't," she replied.

Thus began a conversation that did nothing to persuade Becki that I had paid her. But I had. A man with only $400 in the bank remembers writing a check for $396.

At the same time, the money for my new tires sat in my bank account, untouched, so a seed of doubt sprouted in my mind. I wrote another check, and this time she promptly deposited it into her bank account.

One night, about three months later, as she was about to leave my apartment, she slid her hands into the pockets of her winter coat and found a crinkled piece of paper. Upon removing it, she looked at it with wide eyes and shoved it back into the pocket from whence it came.

"That wouldn't happen to be a check for $396, would it?" I asked.

"Yes . . ." she replied, her eyes fixed on the floor.

I wish to make a distinction here. Even without this black hole business, the expression "out of sight, out of mind" characterizes the way Becki perceives most objects in her environment. If one of our five felines falls asleep on her smartphone, for instance, she forgets about the phone altogether and drives to work without it.

When she sees me using my phone later in the day, she realizes hers is missing, and asks me to help her search for it. My greatest challenge as her husband then, lies in determining whether the phone is lost in space or time.

When I call her phone and cannot hear it ringing or vibrating somewhere in the house, I search space first. I look under cats and couch cushions, and sometimes even rummage through the clutter in her car (although mine is far messier than hers).

All of this assumes that the phone fell off of Becki's radar because she could no longer see it for some reason—a clear case of out of sight, out of mind. If I cannot find her phone in space, however, I must consider the possibility that it may be out of sight because it is *outside of time.*

While it is tempting to see the disappearance of my $396 check as a case of out of sight, out of mind, I would argue otherwise. Becki often hides her hands in her pockets because she comes from Wisconsin, the Midwestern equivalent of Antarctica. If the check had been in Becki's pocket the entire time, she surely would have noticed it before that awkward moment in my apartment.

The check probably took a cue from Wisconsin's motto—"Forward"—and leapt into the future.

I could be wrong about all of this, of course. Becki may simply be a bit like the Absent-Minded Professor—prone to forget little things because her brain is preoccupied with big words like trimethylaminuria.

Thinking this might be the case, I once bought her an electronic key finder that prompts a corresponding key fob to emit a high-pitched beeping sound at the push of a button. As soon as I bought it, I knew it might disappear, too.

Do we need to invest in a key-finder finder as well? I wondered.

I asked Becki to keep the device in our junk drawer so we would always know where to find it. It still resides there, but its batteries died long ago because she used it so often. She wants to replace them herself, but she has yet to do so, and I doubt she ever will. Even if she did, the batteries would probably disappear as soon as she bought them. Few things escape the gravitational pull of my wife, the black hole.

A closing thought: A few months ago I drove my car to the service shop that performs routine maintenance on my car. When I pulled into the parking lot I found that the building no longer existed.

In my astonishment, I sat in my car, staring at the bare ground where the shop once sat. The building—a former Chrysler dealership—had been one in a series of such places on the street, so its absence reminded me of a missing tooth in the mouth of a seven-year-old.

A nearby sign indicated that the service shop's operations had been temporarily relocated to one of the other dealerships on the block. When I visited the shop's new location, I asked the attendant behind the counter what had happened to the old building. He said it had been demolished, and explained that management planned to erect a new one on the site soon.

I believed him until I drove past that plot of land again after the shop finished working on my car. I looked across the street from the barren lot and saw Lawrence's Honda dealership. I thought I remembered Becki taking her Civic there recently for repairs.

It dawned on me in that moment that the woman who loses her car keys daily, and who once misplaced her Honda Civic for a day, might be responsible for the disappearance of the service shop across the street. Sure, the shop's employees had said it had been demolished, but only because no one would believe them if they said, "We came to work one day, and the building just wasn't there!"

Were Becki's powers increasing? Could she really make a building disappear simply by driving past it? I decided to make a few inquiries about the matter.

"How's your car doing these days?" I asked her at dinner that night. "Didn't you just take it in to get something fixed recently?"

"Yeah," she said. "The people at the Honda dealership replaced one of my front wheel bearings."

I had no idea what a wheel bearing was, but it seemed to me she could have been close enough to the service shop across the street to trap it in her temporal vortex. Of course, I had no idea why she spared the Honda dealership, or our house, or any other building in Lawrence, for that matter.

"Did you notice anything... *weird* while you were at the dealership?" I asked.

Like someone saying "Tarnation! The building across the street just vanished into thin air!" I thought.

"Weird? What do you mean?"

"Oh nothing," I said. "Never mind."

I decided not to burden Becki with my suspicions. If she saw the vacant lot, I would simply tell her the building had been demolished. It worked for the shop employees, so I figured it could work for me, too.

In my secret heart, however, I wondered what would happen if the owners built a new structure on that empty plot. Would the old building obliterate the new one when it reappeared after traveling into the future?

As I thought about these things, a Bible verse came to mind. Ecclesiastes 12:13 (KJV) says, "Fear God and keep his commandments, for this is the whole duty of man." As the son of a minister and a Christian, I have often found it difficult to understand how a person can both fear God and love him.

When I think of the way Becki makes things disappear, however, I see how affection and apprehension can coexist in the heart and characterize how one person experiences another.

I see this, and I think I understand—thanks to my wife, the black hole.

"Shoes for My Wife, Secret Centipede,"
digital art by Mark Montgomery.

Putting the "Die" in Diarrhea

★ ★ ★

One morning, when Becki was sitting at the island in our kitchen, eating breakfast and thumbing through a magazine, I made the mistake of asking her what she was reading.

"An article about diarrhea," she said matter-of-factly, as if diarrhea were a subject that could ever be discussed matter-of-factly, let alone at breakfast.

As a physician assistant, Becki is always reading medical magazines, so this revelation should not have surprised me. But somehow, knowing that she was sitting there, eating cereal and reading about diarrhea with clinical detachment, I could not help but laugh.

"It's not funny," she snapped. "Diarrhea can be a serious medical condition, Chad!"

Not funny? I thought. *What the—*

I knew people could die from diarrhea, but it almost never happened in the United States. It was unheard of, and it was therefore unreal to me.

Most of all though, I will never be able to dissociate diarrhea from laughter, thanks to a certain song my peers and I sang on the playground in elementary school. The lyrics address a baseball player who has "the runs" as he runs from one base to another.

When you're heading for first / and your pants begin to burst / diarrhea (clap, clap) / diarrhea (clap, clap).

Yes sir, diarrhea was deadly. I forget the couplet that commemorates the poor player reaching second base, but third—

Well, I remember that one.

When you're sliding into third / and you feel a juicy turd / diarrhea (clap, clap) / diarrhea (clap, clap).

If you ask my inner nine-year-old boy, diarrhea is pretty bulletproof in the funny department. It occurs to me as I write this, however, that Becki may have reacted to my laughter that morning as she did because she has no inner nine-year-old boy. (I suppose it would be weird if she did, come to think of it.) Her inner child is a prim and proper little girl who rolls her hazel eyes at immature inner children like mine.

In addition to being much more mature than I will ever be, Becki has no sense of humor until noon or thereabouts. According to her twin, Katie, Becki has always been "a grouch" in the morning.

During our first year of marriage, in fact, Katie offered to host an Oscar-the-Grouch-themed birthday party for Becki at our house. As much as I enjoyed the idea, I shot it down. I am self-conscious about my own short fuse, and I would react with horror if someone baked a banana-shaped birthday cake in honor of the anger monkey on my back.

I understood Katie's intentions though. For her, loving her twin meant embracing her flaws as well as her finer qualities.

The laughter continued.

"Stop laughing, Chad!" Becki exclaimed. "There's nothing funny about me reading about diarrhea while I eat shredded wheat cereal!"

Wait, wait, wait. Did she say shredded wheat cereal?

How on Earth had I failed to notice that Becki was eating a fibrous cereal that promoted bowel health while reading about bowel infirmity? At that point, in addition to laughing uncontrollably, I began slapping my knee with great gusto.

"Chad, you laugh too much! Stop it!" Becki bellowed. My laughter faded as soon as I saw her icy eyes, which suggested she might slap my face with great gusto if I could not regain my composure.

"I . . . I laugh too much?" I asked in astonishment.

"Yes, you're always laughing, Chad!"

"There's nothing wrong with laughing, you know," I said as I caught my breath. "Did you ever think maybe you're just too serious?"

Early in our marriage, morning episodes like these prompted me to retreat to the basement before the sun rose so I could avoid incurring undue wrath. That time has since become my designated writing time.

The afternoon after this incident, I received a spritely email from Becki. It might as well have been written by a squirrel, so chipper was its tone.

"I love you, Honey! You're the best! You're my favorite!"

I imagined her springing from one branch to another, clutching an acorn with her little limbs. Could the person who had accused me of laughing too much only a matter of hours ago really write an email like this?

It made me wonder if the two of us might have a dynamite discussion about diarrhea in the middle of the day, after her morning moodiness subsides. If I ever attempt to have such a conversation with her, however, I will probably proceed with extreme caution in case I am wrong.

I like to say Becki put the "die" in "diarrhea" that day, but she spared my life and the life of my inner nine-year-old boy as well. I dare not test her again.

When you're sliding into home / and your pants are filled with foam / diarrhea (clap, clap) / diarrhea (clap, clap).

After reading the completed essay, Becki said:

"I still think diarrhea is a serious subject, and should not be taken lightly. I don't have to put the 'die' in diarrhea—it already kills people, Chad."

"Wedlockness," ink illustration by Ben Chlapek.

Before naming this book *Nightmarriage*, I considered titling it *Wedlockness*. Marriage is mysterious, after all, and so is the Loch Ness monster. A better title yet may be *I Love Me Some Em Dashes!*

The Art of the Pity Party, Perfected

★ ★ ★

"The tongue of the wise commends knowledge, but the mouths of fools pour out folly."—Proverbs 15:2 (ESV)

Early in our marriage, after an abysmal day at work, I decided to throw myself a pity party. While sorry soirees such as these tend to be solitary affairs, I wanted Becki to attend mine.

As the only person on God's green Earth who publicly promised to bear with me for better or worse, I thought she might enjoy comforting me in my hour of need. Thinking of how best to bring Becki into my suffering, I considered crafting an invitation.

"Dear Becki," it would read, "You're invited to attend your husband's pity party! Lachrymimosas (orange juice and champagne mixed with human tears) will be provided. Please RSVP. Love, Your Husband."

But I was too depressed to write anything so formal—to write anything at all, for that matter.

"Can you feel sorry for me, Honey?" I asked shortly after she came home from work. "I had a really bad day."

"I'm really not in the mood for that," she replied. "I had a really bad day, too."

RSVP received. I would be the only attendee at my pity party, as Becki apparently planned to host one of her own.

"Well, I could go to Hastings and look at books," I said. "You know—get out of the house and give you some time to yourself. It sounds like you could use it, Hon."

On the surface, this probably seems like a reasonably considerate offer. I had no intention of actually going to Hastings, however—none whatsoever. As an unrepentant homebody, I rarely want to go anywhere, really. When I am depressed, I want to leave even less.

I wanted to mope to my heart's content that night. I wanted to become one with the living room couch. More than anything though, I wanted Becki to collect my tears in test tubes. Without her help, how would I ever make those lachrymimosas?

Knowing that I prefer to stay at home whenever I possibly can, Becki would see my offer to leave the house as a surprising sacrifice of sorts. If I succeeded in sounding sincere, she would appreciate my consideration for her feelings and automatically attune herself to my needs out of a sense of reciprocity.

"Oh, you don't need to go anywhere, Chaddy," she would say. "It was nice of you to offer though. I think you should stay in tonight and let me take care of you."

In the end, I would win her favor without lifting a finger. Even better, in declining my offer, she would feel like a wonderful wife for placing my needs above her own.

Unfortunately, however, fools seldom succeed in crafting foolproof plans.

"You would go to Hastings just give me some time to myself?" she replied, and with far more enthusiasm than I had anticipated. "That sounds wonderful, Chad! Thank you so much! Wow!"

I immediately saw the flaw in my plan. For all Becki knew, I might have relished the idea of leaving the house to look at books at Hastings. I am a writer, after all, and writers tend to be fond of books.

But Hastings also sells CDs, DVDs, and vinyl. As a pop culture junkie, I frequently find myself drawn to that store as if by magnetic forces. Becki knew this, too. *Why* had I offered to go there?

I should have volunteered to visit a place I loathed. A home repair store like Lowe's or Home Depot would have sufficed. Sally's Beauty Supply would have worked nicely, too. I would never end up at home, my wife tending to my workday wounds, if I offered to resign myself to anything other than an evening of unadulterated suffering.

"Actually, I don't really feel like looking at books," I said, backpedaling as best I could. In my bumbling buffoonery, however, I overcompensated. "I think I'd rather sit in the parking lot at Hastings and read in my car."

I think I'd rather sit in the parking lot at Hastings and read in my car? I thought. *Did I just say that out loud? Who says that?!?*

"Okay, go ahead and do that," she said without a moment's hesitation. "I could really use some time to myself. Thanks again, Honey."

"Ahem—I said I'm going to *read* in the *parking lot*," I repeated, emphasizing the especially preposterous parts. "*At Hastings.*" Had I mentioned that I planned to read in the parking lot at Hastings?

"Okay," she continued, already absorbed in the most recent issue of *Vogue* magazine. "You do what you need to do."

"Funny thing, reading in cars," I continued. "I wouldn't really need to leave the house to do that, would I? I could just go down to the garage and . . ."

No dice. No fuzzy dice either.

"I bet I'll be the only guy reading in his car in the parking lot at Hastings," I continued. "Won't that be a hoot?"

It occurred to me at that moment that, if I failed to make good on my offer, my ploy for attention would be revealed for what it was. I had backed myself into a corner or, more accurately, a parking space.

Perhaps Becki saw through my scheming all along. She worked as a nanny in college, and is therefore wise to the wiles of children.

There I was, playing the part of the attention-seeking child who shouts at his parents, "I'm going to run away and you'll never see me again—never EVER!" Like any mother who wants to teach her child that theatrics will not be tolerated, Becki had replied, "Okay, go ahead and do that."

Only a truly foolish child tells his parents he plans to run away and then actually hops a train to the nearest city, riding in a boxcar with a bunch of harmonica-toting hobos. Likewise, only a truly foolish husband tells his wife he plans to read in the parking lot at Hastings and then actually does so.

I could have driven downtown and dug through vinyl at Love Garden, or immersed myself in an independent film at Liberty Hall, or savored a smoke burger and truffle fries at the Burger Stand. Anything would have been better, after all, than sitting in a parking lot, reading a book.

But fifteen minutes later, I sat in my Dodge Stratus in the parking lot outside of Hastings, reading a book.

It was a pity party that was heavy on pity and light on party. This was the case, at least, until I looked up from my reading.

In a car a few spaces away from me sat another man who had apparently resigned himself to the ridiculous fate of reading in the parking lot at Hastings. I suppose no pity party is really a party unless more than one person attends.

I will never know why that man was there, reading—but there he sat all the same. In my mind, we were two monuments to male stupidity. We sat in the parking lot at Hastings like quotation marks on opposite ends of the same sentence: *I think I'd rather sit in the parking lot at Hastings and read in my car.*

After a seeming eternity elapsed, I drove home. Unlike mine, Becki's pity party had been a smashing success, as she was in a much happier headspace. A week later, I told her about the other man who had been reading in his car that night.

"Reading in his car?" she said. "In a parking lot? Why would he do that? What on Earth are you talking about?"

Unlike my wife, I would never forget that night. If I did, I would surely end up sitting in my Stratus, staring at a book all over again. On the other hand, if I happen to find myself in a parking lot populated by fellow page-turning fools, at least I will not be alone in my folly.

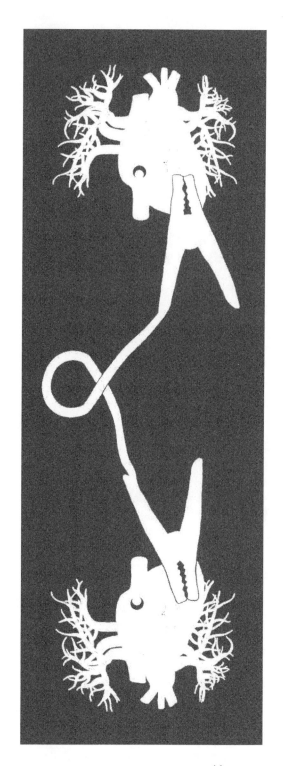

"Hearts and Jumper Cables," mixed media by Danny Joe Gibson.

Hearts and Jumper Cables

★ ★ ★

Four months into our marriage, Becki and I encountered an omen under the hood of my Dodge Stratus. People rarely say good things about Dodges, so it seemed strangely appropriate that mine would want to play the part of the woeful, unwanted prophet.[13]

---

[13] My car comes from a long line of Dodge descendants. First came my parents' Reliant K. In the end, it was a lemon, and they were tempted to juice it and recoup the money they spent on it with a street-side lemonade stand.

After the Reliant K, they opted for an Aries K, which looked exactly like the lemon that preceded it. The summer before I became a sophomore in college, it became my first car. I loved that boxy beast even though it failed me on multiple occasions.

By the time I sold it, it had a cracked engine block and no air conditioning. Whenever it threatened to overheat on the road, I turned the heater on, forcing coolant to circulate through the engine. This meant none of my friends asked me for rides during the summer months.

Then there was my '93 Spirit, which blew a head gasket and finally gave up the ghost at a little over 110,000 miles.

When I bought my 2003 Stratus, I did so with great fondness in my heart for Dodges despite my previous experiences with the brand. Becki, who drives a Honda Civic, looks upon my Stratus with skepticism.

"I hope your car lasts awhile, Chad," she says. "I mean, it's a Dodge, so it's probably not going be around for too long, but I hope I'm wrong."

"Oh, don't worry," I reply. "My last Dodge lasted 110,000 miles, and I only have 72,000 on the Stratus."

Becki is perplexed by this because, in human years, her car will live to be the age of Methuselah. She cannot understand why I find it acceptable for a car to die at such a young age.

For a time after we married, I parked my car in the driveway because the mechanism that opened the door on my side of the garage had broken. We fixed the problem in a hurry, however, after mice or squirrels or children with pica made a meal out of the spark plug wires that ran across my engine block.

Without these wires, my car began to convulse as soon as I started it. Sitting in the driver's seat, I felt like a can of paint in a mixing machine might if it were sentient.

When I lifted the hood to look for the cause of the quaking, I saw sparks shooting across the engine block. With wide eyes and fumbling fingers, I dialed AAA's number and told the operator my Stratus needed to be towed for repairs.

Despite having two degrees in communication studies, I never learned to speak anything other than a pidgin version of the "automobilese" needed to communicate effectively with tow truck drivers, car mechanics, and the like.

"Sparks bad," I said in clunky caveman-speak to the tow truck driver when he arrived. "Bad, bad—very bad sparks! Tow truck big. Tow truck good—not bad!"

Immediately recognizing that I lacked proficiency in automobilese, he responded with a nod and towed me to the auto shop that regularly serviced my Stratus—and this was long before my wife, the black hole, made that place disappear. Much to my surprise, the mechanic at the shop spoke an automobilese-English hybrid I could actually understand for the most part.

"You got a four-cylinder engine," he said, "and because the squirrels or whatever ate your wires, you're only runnin' on two. Vermin'll eat anything, ya know?"

But what kind of squirrel would eat wires? I wondered. I immediately imagined a cyborg squirrel stuffing its cheeks with the kinds of nuts people pair with bolts.

"Runnin' on two cylinders'll make your car shake like that, see?"

"I see," I said—and I think I did, for the most part.

As I thought about what I had seen under the hood that day, it occurred to me that, in marriage, two hearts are connected as if by wires—or maybe something more like jumper cables. When we tie the knot, we tether our hearts together, too, and feed off of one another accordingly. Becki boosts my mood, for example, whenever she is happy.

With regard to the ties that bind two hearts together in marriage, the shower of sparks under the hood of my Stratus spoke a prophetic message loud and clear that day: Beware the squirrels of selfishness, stress, and strife, for they feed on the cables that connect one heart to another.

Two months later, those squirrels would visit Becki and me.

A few days after Christmas, Becki and I watched *The Hangover* with our friends Brandon and Joanna, whose hearts are likewise joined by jumper cables. We often while away the hours with "Branjo," as we refer to them collectively—listening to records, watching movies, and partaking of Joanna's homemade pretzels and beer-cheese dipping sauce.

Branjo live in a duplex only a few miles from our house, so when we left their place that night at around 10:00 p.m., we assumed we would be home in a matter of minutes. We had a white Christmas in Lawrence that year, however, and snow was falling again as we drove home. Being a native Missourian, I drove with excess caution as only people who never drive in snow do.

"Snow bad," I said to Becki in pidgin automobilese. "Very bad snow."

Everyone knows that Wisconsinites are born to abominable snowmen doctors in hospitals made of ice, so winter weather does not faze them in the least. Becki exercised great restraint then, when she refrained from ridiculing my driving as I slogged through the snow that night.

Then it happened.

My vision impaired by the snowfall, I steered my Stratus into a hotel parking lot instead of onto the exit ramp that would have led us to our cozy home. Little did I know upon pulling into that lot that I would not leave it for over two hours, and I would do so without my wife.

Stupid pothole.

It was deep and wide, like the Sunday school song. My front left tire squealed in panic as it spun against the hole's icy lining, spraying slush all over the underside of my car.

When Becki realized we were stranded, the squirrels that feast upon the cables connecting man and wife made a meal out of ours.

"I can't *believe* you did this," Becki bellowed. "You could've avoided this, but you just drove *right* into that pothole! *Let's just park in a pothole, why don't we?*"

"I didn't see it, Honey," I said. "I just . . . I was driving and—"

"—and *you* don't know how to drive in this weather, Chad! *I do.* I'm from Wisconsin, where there's lots of *snow!* We *know* how to drive in the *snow* in Wisconsin!"

"Gee," I said in terror and timidity, "I can't believe this hotel hasn't done something about this hole. We should really talk to their management about this." But my attempt to transfer the blame to the hotel's owners failed.

I climbed out of the car and pushed on the bumper while Becki gunned the gas pedal. The wheel continued to spin and squeal.

Why is it that some surprises are good and others are bad? I wondered as I pushed, the soles of my feet failing to find traction on the snowy surface of the parking lot. *Surprise birthday parties are good, but surprise potholes are bad. Why does life have to be so confusing?*

Bewildered, I climbed back into the car, aware that we were stranded in a hotel parking lot because of me.

"I'm going to walk home, Chad," Becki said.

"Wait—you're going to walk home at night when it's snowing and everything's covered in ice?"

"Yep," she replied, flames of fury flashing in her eyes as she slammed the door behind her.

As she disappeared into the night, I pictured her wandering with the wives of all of the other men in Lawrence who parked their Dodge Strata[14] in potholes in hotel parking lots. I heard the sound of a thousand tires spinning and squealing, a thousand men sputtering profanity, and a thousand fingers with manicured nails dialing divorce lawyers.

I called Brandon, thinking he might still be awake. I would have called AAA, but I figured the wait would have been a long one considering the road conditions.

---

[14] This is the plural form of "Stratus," right?

I knew Brandon, the Human Swiss Army Knife, would be able to help. He always possesses the tools needed to remedy any problem. He owns so many, in fact, that he parks his Ford Focus in the driveway because his garage has been overrun by things like ratchets, hatchets, hammers, and hacksaws.

I thought Brandon might be awake because people who hope to earn PhDs in philosophy seldom rest. As of this writing, he is about to defend his doctoral dissertation. At the time of this incident, however, he still had a fair amount of coursework to complete. Like his garage, his brain remains overstuffed, but with the words of dead philosophers instead of ballpeen hammers and band saws.

Brandon answered his phone and arrived on the scene in minutes. After much strategizing, spinning, squealing, and swearing, however, we called AAA. Neither tools nor the logic of Ludwig Wittgenstein, Brandon's favorite philosopher, could set my Stratus free.

Brandon volunteered to wait with me until the tow truck arrived. Around this time, Becki reappeared outside of the car. I could be wrong, but I think she returned because the cold reminded her of home—both the one she left when she moved from Wisconsin to Kansas, and the one she shared with her hapless husband.

Brandon offered to drive her home, and she accepted without argument. Being the faithful friend he is, he returned to the hotel parking lot to wait with me after dropping her off. We sat in the arctic dark and talked about some of our favorite subjects: artificial intelligence, baseball, and science-fiction films. The AAA tow truck arrived shortly thereafter and plucked my Dodge Stratus from the perilous pothole with embarrassing ease.

After I bid Brandon goodnight, I headed home and found all the lights off when I arrived. I tiptoed up the stairs and down the hallway, hoping to avoid awakening my weary wife.

When I entered our bedroom I expected it to feel like an icebox, but Becki's heart had thawed considerably by the time I came home. I suppose love can be jump-started easily enough when the cables joining a couple's hearts are reinforced with commitment. As long as we remained committed, our marriage would be squirrel-proof.

"I know you didn't mean to get your car stuck in that pothole, Honey," she said. "I'm sorry I yelled at you."

"Really?" I said.

"Really, Chaddy."

"Forgiveness good. Pothole bad," I said. "Very bad pothole. Marriage good."

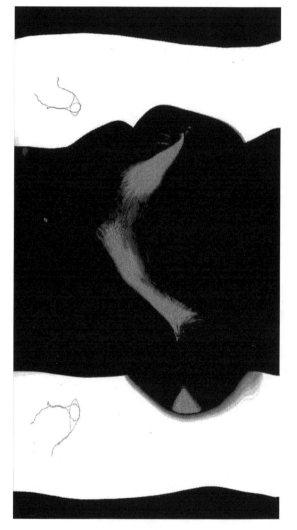

"Transmission Impossible," mixed media by Danny Joe Gibson.

Dew Ewe Here Watt Eye Hear?

★ ★ ★

Dedicated to Dr. John S. Bourhis and Dr. Charlene Berquist

Husband-wife duo Noël Regney and Gloria Shayne wrote the Christmas classic "Do You Hear What I Hear?" as a prayer for peace in response to the Cuban Missile Crisis in 1962. To my ears, however, the refrains that repeat throughout the song seem like they might be suited for preventing prospective marital meltdowns, too.

Consider the song lyric, "Do you see what I see?" If Becki would ask herself if I can see what she sees at any given time, she would refrain from asking questions like, "Chad, what do you think of this?" when I am in another room.

"What's 'this'?" I reply. "I can't see 'this,' so I have *no* idea what you're talking about, Honey."

"Oh, you know what I mean!" she replies.

But I never do. If I had a nickel for every time Becki said things like this, I would have enough money to buy that thing over there. (See what I just did?)

While the Cuban Missile Crisis never escalated into nuclear war, Regney and Shayne's marriage went kablooey in 1973. Apparently, the writers of "Do You Hear What I Hear?" both heard the sound of their marriage disintegrating.

Becki and I never want to hear that sound. We know that the smallest misunderstandings can become the biggest sources of tension in a marriage, creating a Cold War dynamic between two people who have promised to love one another unto death.

In order to preserve the peace in our household then, I find myself attempting to troubleshoot marital miscommunications whenever they arise. Like a therapist who constantly talks to his wife about the importance of feelings, my two degrees in communication studies compel me to bombard Becki with talk about talk all the time.[15]

"Honey, when you say 'What do you think of this?' and I'm not in the room," I explain, "I have no visual referent to pair with the word 'this.' Don't you see?" I am the human equivalent of a communication textbook sometimes, and probably one Becki wishes she could shut or sell.

In the end, I only want Becki and me to understand one another as well as we possibly can. Singer-songwriter Sufjan Stevens knows what I mean. In his 2012 cover of "Do You Hear What I Hear?" he added a question to the lyric, and it probes the heart of mutual understanding in marriage: "Do you feel what I feel?"

Becki and I want to be able to answer this question in the affirmative, so she tries to put herself in my loafers, and I try to put myself in her flats, high heels, sandals, and sneakers. We want our marriage to last, and we believe the road to marital longevity is paved with empathy.

Unfortunately, this road, like certain hotel parking lots, happens to be riddled with potholes. Becki and I may share a common language, after all, but we can speak the same sentence and mean two totally different things. When semantics sideline us, a better question—and my own addition to Regney and Shayne's classic, I suppose—is "Do you mean what I think you mean?"

On one memorable occasion, for instance, as we drove past a Steak 'n Shake, Becki exclaimed, "Ooh, I want a shake!"

---

[15] Upon reading this sentence, Becki said, "Oh, it's so true."

It seemed like such a simple statement.

I signaled to turn, but before I could pull into the restaurant parking lot, Becki grabbed my arm and said, "No, Chad—I don't want a shake! Keep driving!"

But she said she wanted a shake, I thought to myself. *How could she want a shake, but not want one, too?*

When I asked Becki about this apparent contradiction, she said she sometimes vocalizes fleeting wishes without ever intending to fulfill them. I told her this reminded me of Psalm 55:6 (NIV), in which the Psalmist writes, "Oh, that I had the wings of a dove! I would fly away and be at rest." The Psalmist obviously does not mean this statement literally, as a human being could never achieve lift with wings as small as a dove's. Sometimes expressing a desire is enough.

In light of this information, when Becki says, "I want a shake," she means, "A shake sounds good, but I don't really *need* one. I just need to tell you what I'm craving, Chad. You're my husband, so I know you care how I feel."

Other times, when Becki says, "I want a shake," it means she wants a shake. Using the same phrase to vocalize desires that oppose one another makes it seem like my wife speaks a language in which one expression stands for both "yes" and "no."

Early in our marriage, Becki and I developed something like communication shorthand for situations such as these. When Becki says she wants something, but is only vocalizing one of her fleeting wishes, she tells me what she wants and then follows this proclamation with the phrase, "Steak 'n Shake."

If we are shopping in a clothing store then, and she likes a dress but has no intention of purchasing it, she says, "I want that dress. Steak 'n Shake." Sometimes she omits the first part of the statement, points to the dress, and says only "Steak 'n Shake." I hear these words, and know what Becki means. When Becki looks at me and sings "Do you know what I know?" along with Bing Crosby's recording of Regney and Shayne's classic, I can say, "I do!"

But "Steak 'n Shake" is not a communication cure-all. If only it were!

When Becki and I first married, I saw her perusing *People* magazine's website on more than one occasion. When she came down with the flu, I bought the latest issue of the magazine for her in an attempt to assuage her affliction. As soon as I handed it to her, however, she said, "Oh, if you're going to bring me a magazine, you should really bring me *Vogue*."

"Listen to what I s-a-y-y-y-y-y," the song goes.

Not long after she set me straight about her preferred reading material, a coupon for a one-year, fifteen-dollar subscription to *Vogue* magically materialized in our mailbox. I filled it out, mailed it, tried to keep it secret, and failed miserably.

"O-o-o-o-h, you'll never guess what I did!" I said. "I subscribed you to *Vogue*!"

In other words, *I listened to what s-h-e-e-e-e-e said . . .*

"You subscribed me to *Vogue*?" she said, mystified. "Why would you do that? I don't want that, Chad."

"But you said you wanted *Vogue* instead of *People* when—"

"Yeah, I said that when I was sick."

Do you mean what I think you mean?

"I'm not sure what that has to do with anything," I said, "but if you have a subscription, you'll always have a *Vogue* magazine nearby when you're sick. Plus, if you get sick—let's say four times in a year—and I buy you four copies of *Vogue* from the store at five dollars a copy, it's going to cost more than a year's subscription."

"I want you to cancel the subscription, Chad," she said.

Again, I listened to what she said, and attempted to cancel the subscription. A week later, the first issue of the magazine appeared in our mailbox. Apparently, subscription cancellations were not en vogue at *Vogue* that year.

"You know," she said, a smile spreading across her face as she stared at that rogue copy of *Vogue*, "I guess you don't have to cancel that subscription after all, Honey."

The magazines kept coming. The following year, when it came time to renew, she asked if we were going to continue receiving *Vogue*.

"Already renewed your subscription," I said. She smiled and walked away without saying anything, but I knew she had just renewed her commitment to our marriage.

Another time, I returned from picking up carryout pizza only to hear Becki ask if I brought any ranch dipping sauce home for her.

"Why would I do that?" I asked. "You don't even *like* ranch dressing."

I knew this to be true. How could Becki not know this, too? This was a case of "Do you know what I know?" if ever there was one.

I liked dipping my pizza in ranch dressing, but I had never seen Becki do it. Perhaps in some hidden valley in her brain, there was a part of her that liked ranch dressing, but I was unfamiliar with that place. I had never visited that valley.

"It's not that I don't like ranch at all, Chad," she said. "I like it sometimes. Next time you get pizza, bring back some ranch dressing for me, okay?"

The next time we ordered carryout pizza, I returned home with a tiny tub of ranch just for her. She had not asked for it that day, but I remembered the conversation we had the last time I brought pizza home.

"You brought me ranch dressing?" she asked, incensed by my apparent idiocy. "But why? You know I don't like ranch dressing."

As I suspected in the first place.

Seeing what Becki sees, hearing what she hears, knowing what she knows, and listening to what she says will never ensure that our communication will be free of confusion. I sometimes think I have my wife all figured out, but then she throws me a verbal curveball, and I become a student of her ways all over again. In my confused state, I fumble and utter phrases like "Do you want ranch dressing on your *Vogue* magazine or not?"

While our marital miscommunications sometimes frustrate me, I have come to see them as an amusing aspect of marriage. Everyone says two become one in marriage, but Becki and I have yet to successfully merge our minds. We can, however, look into each other's eyes and sing "Are you as confused as I am?" to the tune of Regney and Shayne's song. This we can do together—and we can both reply, "Yes."

"There Will Be Consequences,"
ink illustration by Megan Frauenhoffer.

Knives and Wives

★ ★ ★

"Chad, what was the name of that woman?" Becki asked one night as we climbed into bed. "You know, the one who cut off her husband's penis with a knife?"

This question came out of absolutely nowhere.

"Why do you want to know?" I said, my voice cracking. What kinds of evil eggs were hatching in her brain?

"I just want to know," she replied. "What was her name again? Erma Bombeck?"

Erma Bombeck? I thought. *No. Dear goodness, no. Wow.*

"No, Hon," I said. "Erma Bombeck was a writer—a humorist. She wrote the book *If Life is a Bowl of Cherries, What Am I Doing in the Pits?* Definitely nothing about penises in there—at least as far as I know. I haven't read it. I think my grandma Ruthie owned it."

"Oh," she said.

"I think you're thinking of Lorena Bobbitt."

"Oh right! Bobbitt!" She squealed. "Erma Bombeck. Lorena Bobbitt. I see how I got it wrong!"

I don't, I thought.

I slept with one eye open for a long time after that.

"Michael Jackson, King of Pop (Not to Be Confused with 'King of Soda')," watercolor by BARRR.

"Gary Coleman in Cowboy Hat," watercolor by BARRR.

Honeymoonwalking (To Jail)

★ ★ ★

"I have to write about it," I whispered to Becki under my breath as we waited in line to check out at Hastings.

"Don't you *dare* write about it," Becki whispered. "If you do, people will think we're racists, Chad."

We always have time to talk in the queue at Hastings. Despite the store's name, none of the clerks who staff the registers know the meaning of haste.

"But we're not racists," I replied a little louder than I intended.

"Yes, but people will *think* we are, Chad." The cashier eyed us with suspicion and rang up the stack of used CDs I rescued from the clearance rack.

Great, I thought. *The cashier's going to think we're racists* and *cheap.*

Our conversation began the moment we saw the twenty-fifth anniversary edition of *Thriller* on vinyl in the music section of the store. As we looked at the album cover, Becki and I both felt Michael Jackson's image staring at us with accusatory eyes.

"I just can't keep quiet anymore," I said upon seeing the record, my heart throbbing to the tempo of "Beat It." "How can *you*, Honey? I mean, Michael Jackson died on our honeymoon, and now every time our anniversary approaches, another African-American celebrity dies!"

I think that pretty much says it all—does it not?

It all began on June 20, 2009, when Becki and I exchanged rings and vows at First Baptist Church in Lawrence, Kansas. My father presided over the ceremony.

Five days later, Michael Jackson died while we honeymooned in Kansas City. He moonwalked out of this life the same week we walked down the aisle to celebrate the kind of bond that powers pop songs like Jackson's "The Way You Make Me Feel."

How did it make us feel when Jackson died during our honeymoon? Well—weird, for starters. We never expected to forever associate newlywed bliss with the death of *the* icon that dominated American culture during our childhoods.

Becki and I saw the news of Jackson's passing on a TV hanging in a store window at the Crown Center shopping complex in downtown Kansas City. We were on our way to see Ron Simonian's play, *Desperate Times-Desperate Measures*, at the Off Center Theatre on the third floor of the main building when the screen captured our attention.

The news crawled across the bottom of the screen like a funeral procession. How fitting that we should find out about the death of a king in a place called Crown Center!

In the wake of his passing, the King of Pop's subjects—record buyers in every nation—suddenly seemed to remember how Michael Jackson made them feel before scandals called his crown into question.

"I can't believe he died on our honeymoon," I said to Becki the next morning over continental breakfast in the lobby of our hotel. "I feel like it's our fault somehow. I mean, we go our whole lives without honeymooning, and Michael Jackson's fine. Then we honeymoon, and he's dead."

"That's ridiculous, Chad," Becki said. "We didn't kill Michael Jackson."

"I don't think you understand what I mean," I said. "This may sound like a tangent, but—you know I used to be a big baseball fan, right?"

"Yes, unfortunately," she replied.

"Are you saying 'unfortunately' because of my baseball card collection?" I asked. I had moved all of my belongings into our house the week before we wed, including enough storage boxes to hold some 14,000 cards.

"You assume correctly."

"Okay, well when I was a kid, my friends and I watched Royals baseball on TV all the time. But if we missed a game and the Royals lost, we'd say something like, 'I knew I shouldn't have missed that game. Every time I miss a game, they lose!' Do you know what I mean?"

Becki's blank expression said she did not.

"I assume the people in Wisconsin say similar things about the Packers," I continued.

"Oh, 'da Pack! Right—yes, I suppose they do," she said. "I had no idea what you were talking about for a minute there. But... what on Earth does all of this have to do with Michael Jackson dying on our honeymoon?"

"Well, I fell out of love with baseball during the players' strike of 1994, and I've often told people the Royals stopped playing quality ball when I stopped watching the sport. I know it's magical thinking, but—"

"So let me get this straight," she interjected. "You're saying that Michael Jackson died because we honeymooned, and your rationale for this is rooted in . . . magical thinking?"

"Yes," I said. "Magical thinking."

"Okay—whatever you say, Chad," Becki said, returning her focus to her breakfast.

I knew no causal link actually existed between our honeymoon and the King of Pop's passing. But when another African-American celebrity died a year later, I thought perhaps I had been wrong.

To truly understand the connection I am about to make, the reader should know that Becki and I often celebrate birthdays and holidays early. We can never wait; the excitement proves too much to bear. The first year of our marriage, for example, we exchanged Christmas presents before Thanksgiving.

So when Gary Coleman died on May 28, 2010, less than a month before our first anniversary, we were already celebrating.[16] When I read of Coleman's death then, I immediately thought of Michael Jackson's the year before.

"This is just too weird," I said to Becki. "First Michael Jackson dies on our honeymoon, and then Gary Coleman dies before our first anniversary."

"Yeah—almost an entire *month* before our first anniversary," Becki said. "I'm not sure Gary Coleman's death has anything in common with Michael Jackson's, Chad."

"But we've been celebrating our anniversary for almost a week now, haven't we?"

---

[16] The anniversary card I made Becki for our first anniversary is featured in Appendix B as Exhibit 1.

"Yes, but—"

"You know what's even weirder?" I asked. "I associated Michael Jackson and Gary Coleman in my mind before either of them died, and now I associate them in death, too."

"Wait a second," she interrupted. "Why did you associate them with each other before they died? Just because they were African-American celebrities that were popular in the '80s?"

"Well, that's part of it," I said. "Then there's the matter of Michael Jackson living at a place called Neverland. I don't know about you, but I always thought of Gary Coleman as a real-life Peter Pan because of his medical problems. I mean, he stopped growing at 4' 7" and had sort of a childlike appearance throughout his life, right?"

"Oddly enough, that sort of makes sense," Becki said.

"But there's even more to it than that," I continued. "Bear with me for a minute here, okay?"

"Okay . . ."

"Both of them were popular when my sister Alyssa and I were growing up, but we never watched *Diff'rent Strokes* or listened to Michael Jackson's music. They just weren't on my family's radar. But I knew who Gary Coleman and Michael Jackson were because my classmates would talk about them, you know? They'd use one of Gary Coleman's catch phrases from the show, or they'd moonwalk down the hall at school."

"But your parents *did* let you listen to music and watch TV, right?"

"Oh yes—most definitely," I said. "We watched *Growing Pains*, *Who's the Boss*, and *The Cosby Show* every week. Those were our favorite shows. For all I know, maybe we didn't watch *Diff'rent*

Strokes because it came on at the same time as one of those shows. I really couldn't say."

"So you're basically saying you also associate Michael Jackson with Gary Coleman because neither of them were in your life, but you knew about them . . ."

". . . and that made me curious about them. That made them seem kind of mysterious and 'other' to me, I think."

"I can see how your family might have missed out on *Diff'rent Strokes*, but why didn't you listen to Michael Jackson?" she asked.

I remember hearing Jackson's *Thriller* album at the birthday party of a grade school classmate of mine in 1983 at the age of five. It was probably the only time I heard it as a child. The King of Pop's reign did not extend to the Johnston household because we only worshipped the King of Kings.[17]

As Christians, we listened exclusively to Contemporary Christian Music (CCM). When my sister Alyssa was seven and I was eleven, she told our parents she wanted to see Michael Jackson in concert. They had no idea how to respond, and neither did I.

---

[17] In sixth grade, my classmates belonged to two cliques: Skaters and bikers. I pledged allegiance to the skaters because I thought bicycles were boring. My mom bought me a generic skateboard from SEARS to help me fit in at school. I made the mistake of telling my peers about it.

"You have a SEARS skateboard? That's lame. Mine's a Powell Peralta board. *Powell Peralta rules!*" said one overzealous skater named Sean.

When I told my mother about this, she said, "Next time he says that to you, say 'No, Sean. Jesus rules!'"

I may or may not have said this to Sean. I honestly cannot recall. But one thing is for certain: Michael Jackson would never be the king of anything at our house if Mom had anything to say about it.

"You want to see Michael Jackson in concert?" I asked Alyssa. "But why?" We had CCM artists like Amy Grant, David Meece, and Carman to call our own. Why did she need Michael Jackson, too?

I had nothing against Michael Jackson, of course, but I knew that songs like "Beat It," "Billie Jean," and "Thriller" made no mention of Jesus or God or anything even vaguely Sunday School-ish.

I could have been wrong about this, of course.

Having only heard "Billie Jean" a few times as a boy, I thought the song was about a boy named Billie Jean who was not Michael Jackson's son. I knew nothing about paternity disputes, let alone how men became fathers, so this seemed like a peculiar premise for a song to me.

Carman sang about someone's son, too—and one whose paternity remains in dispute for many. In his spoken word epic, "The Champion," the Son of God and Satan square-off in a cosmic boxing ring. God plays the part of referee, and allows Satan to land a fatal blow. But Jesus does not remain dead for long. Instead of counting to ten to signify Satan's victory, God counts backwards from ten as if he is undoing the Devil's deathblow. In the end, Jesus emerges victorious, and Satan becomes the vanquished villain.

I can still hear Carman shouting the final words of the song: "And Jesus . . . IS . . . the CHAMPION (Echo: Champion-champion-champion)!!!"

As a child, this song thrilled me more than anything I ever heard by Michael Jackson. Ten years later or thereabouts, I would learn that the dead rose from the grave in Jackson's "Thriller" video, too. But none of those dancing zombies had ever endeavored to save humanity. That being said, "The Champion" may well be the greatest novelty song of all time—a musical *Rocky* for the religious set that remains as absurd as it is inspiring.[18]

"What can Michael Jackson do that Carman can't do better?" I asked Alyssa. Having spent a decade on this spinning orb, I thought I knew a thing or two about pop culture.

Alyssa never mentioned Michael Jackson again—at least as far as I can remember. A few decades later, however, her husband Paul introduced her to the music of Bruce Springsteen, whose songs likewise never spun on turntables or played on cassette decks at our house.

I only knew about The Boss as a boy because his song, "Born in the U. S. A.," had been appropriated by Ronald Reagan for his reelection campaign in 1984. I championed Reagan as a six-year-old because my classmate Jason, who would later become a convict, told me Walter Mondale would spread cancer across America if elected. Oh, the things we accept uncritically as children!

When Springsteen's African-American saxophonist, Clarence Clemons, passed away on June 18, 2011—two days before Becki and I celebrated our second anniversary—I knew I needed to express my condolences to Paul and Alyssa. I also knew Becki and I needed to have a talk.

I had begun to believe she was right about Gary Coleman. He had been a statistical outlier, dying almost a month before our anniversary, so maybe his death had nothing in common with Michael Jackson's. But Clarence Clemons died close enough to our anniversary that even Becki could not chalk it up to chance.

"Why does this keep happening?" she asked upon hearing of his passing. "Michael Jackson on our honeymoon, and then Gary

---

[18] Carman later starred as a boxer in a film, also titled *The Champion*. I have not seen it. It has an 11% rating on Rotten Tomatoes—an irrefutably rotten ranking.

Coleman before our first anniversary . . . Oh, Chad—who's going to die *next* year?!?"

"I know," I replied. "I'm concerned, too. I think I should write about this, Honey—maybe a bloated essay with a number of seemingly inconsequential tangents. What do you think?"

"Well, I don't know if we want to call unnecessary attention to ourselves, you know?" she replied. "I mean, people might think we're racists or even worse—that we're accessories to murder."

"You might be right," I said. "But at the same time, if more African-American celebrities die on or around our anniversaries in the future, we're going to feel partially responsible for their deaths if we don't issue some kind of warning. And if we don't call attention to this phenomenon, someone else probably will. I mean, if some Columbo comes along and puts the pieces of this puzzle together . . . well, we're doomed."

Of course, Peter Falk, who played the eponymous character on *Columbo*, would never find us out. He died on June 23, 2011—five days after Clarence Clemons passed away. I promise we did not murder him.

The week before Clarence Clemons died, Becki and I visited Crown Center again—this time to celebrate our second anniversary. We had tickets to a theatrical performance of *The 39 Steps*, based on both the John Buchan book and the Alfred Hitchcock film of the same name, at the American Heartland Theatre.

As we strolled through Crown Center that evening, we encountered the image of Michael Jackson outside of the theater in the form of a poster for a live performance of *The Wiz*. The King of Pop had played the Scarecrow in Sidney Lumet's cinematic adaptation of the musical in 1978—the year I was born. I could not help but wonder if this poster had some special significance for Becki and me, considering our history with Jackson.

As we waited to be seated for *The 39 Steps*, my OCD brain began processing information—reviewing the facts, connecting the dots, and so forth. For instance, "I was born in '78, and half of seventy-eight is thirty-nine . . . like *The 39 Steps*." And "I own Hitchcock's version of *The 39 Steps*, and it's in black and white. Oh holy cow—Michael Jackson was black, and then he became white!"

I began mapping all of these correlations out on scrap paper as follows:

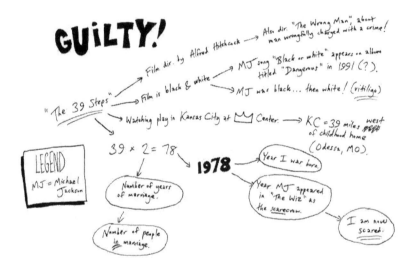

It was evidence—at least in a courtroom that accepts magical thinking as admissible evidence—that could link us to the death of Michael Jackson.

"You see, Your Honor, thirty-nine times two is seventy-eight, and this Johnston fellow was born in 1978," the court-appointed numerologist would explain. "We multiply times two, of course, because Chad and Becki count as two people even though they are one in marriage."

It would be a little more difficult to establish numerical linkage to Gary Coleman's death. For Clarence Clemons, however, he would only need to play Bruce Springsteen's "American Skin (41 Shots)" for the judge and jury—a song that features Clemons on saxophone.

"It's about a man named Amadou Bailo Diallo—a black man from Guinea," the numerologist would continue. "When four members of NYPD blue mistook him for a wanted serial rapist and confronted him, Diallo pulled his wallet from his pocket to identify himself. But the police, mistaking the wallet for a gun, fired forty-one shots at him, hitting him nineteen times. Forty-one shots minus two—again, because Chad and Becki are two even though they are one—equals thirty-nine. I think you see how this all fits together, Your Honor."

The jury would hang on the numerologist's every word. Becki and I would probably hang, too, if we could not prove our innocence.

"But we can also subtract two because Mr. Clemons died *two* days before their *second* anniversary. Too many twos to be a matter of coincidence, wouldn't you say? All of this numerical information constitutes a growing pool of evidence implicating Mr. and Mrs. Johnston in the deaths of multiple African-American celebrities."

Becki and I were only thirty-nine steps away from a conviction, and we knew it.

In 2012, three days before our third anniversary, and three years after the King of Pop's passing, another African-American King died. This one survived being brutally beaten by two Los Angeles police officers on March 3, 1991, and asked America, "Can we all get along?" On June 17, 2012, Rodney King's fiancée found his body at the bottom of his swimming pool. He was only forty-seven.

Not even Matlock could convince a judge we had nothing to do with King's death. Of course, we could hardly hire him to defend us since Andy Griffith, who played Matlock, died on July 3, 2012—only a few weeks after King's passing and our third anniversary.

"What will we do if the police arrest us in connection with all these deaths?" I imagined Becki asking me.

"Well, I think my Stevie Wonder records would convince a judge that we're not racists, Honey," I said.

In 2012, I bought three Stevie Wonder albums: 1973's *Innervisions*, 1974's *Fulfillingness' First Finale*, and 1976's *Songs in the Key of Life*. I mention these purchases because every white person knows, after all, that owning music made by members of other races is tantamount to embracing racial diversity.[19]

"I mean, white people who are racists don't own Stevie Wonder records, right?" I continued. "And white people who aren't racists simply don't kill African-American celebrities, do they? It's that simple."

"But Chad, you bought those albums last year—well after Michael Jackson, Gary Coleman, and Clarence Clemons passed away," the version of Becki in my mind said.

"I don't follow. What's your point?"

"Chad, it might look like you bought those albums because you wanted to give the judge and jury the *impression* that you're not a racist."

"Oh, right," I said. I was as blind as Stevie Wonder when it came to seeing this gaping hole in my logic.

---

[19] I can only hope this is true. In addition to my Stevie Wonder albums, I am a huge fan of Arthur Lee and his band Love. I bought my first Miles Davis record last year, too. As John Cusack's character Rob Gordon says in the film *High Fidelity*, "I haven't quite absorbed that one yet."

"Why *did* you buy those Stevie Wonder records, Chad?" Becki asked.

"Well, his song, 'I Believe (When I Fall in Love It Will Be Forever),' plays over the credits of the film *High Fidelity*, and—"

"I love that movie!"

"—and I just loved that song. I mean, I loved that movie, too—I'm still obsessed with it. But that song piqued my interest in Stevie Wonder's music."

"Well, maybe we can use those albums after all," Becki continued. "But we should still build the strongest case we can. What else have you got?"

As I thought about the passing of the King of Pop and another king named Rodney, I thought of that kingly baseball team I watched as a boy with my friends, and it occurred to me that perhaps they could clear our good name.

As kings go, the Royals remain blue-blooded in name only, of course. They are baseball kings without crowns who are content to cling to the lowest rung on the American League ladder.

I grew up in Odessa, Missouri, a mere thirty-nine miles east of Kansas City—again, the number thirty-nine makes an appearance in our story! Because of my proximity to the Royals' hometown, I thought of them as my team when I was younger. Royals legend George Brett was also born only two weeks before my mom, which made him seem like he could almost be her twin brother.

"I hate to bring up my baseball cards again, but I think they can help us," I said to the version of Becki in my brain.

"They can help us? How? By selling themselves on eBay so we'll have room to store other things in the house?"

"No, seriously—listen to me," I replied. "My baseball cards might double as Get-Out-of-Jail-Free cards!"

I explained that I fell in love with baseball the year the Royals won the World Series in 1985—the same year Carman released his album, *The Champion*. A coincidence? I think not. If the Royals had any sense, they would have hired Carman to announce their victory at the end of the series: "And the Royals . . . ARE . . . the CHAMPIONS [Echo: Champions-champions-champions]!!!"

As I became aware of baseball that year, part of my love for the sport came from seeing people of different races getting along just fine. African-American men like Frank White,[20] Lonnie Smith, and Willie Wilson, and white men like George Brett, Bret Saberhagen, and Bud Black[21] relied on one another on the playing field in a way that would have made yet another king—Martin Luther King, Jr.— proud.

My baseball cards reflected this appreciation for racial diversity, and any judge would agree. I was certain of it.

"Okay, but what cards would you use to strengthen our case?" Becki asked in my mind. "No one has the time to thumb through thousands of baseball cards in a court of law, Chad."

"Well, I have the complete set of Topps baseball cards from 1986," I replied. "That was back when Topps was the dominant baseball card brand, too. The Royals featured in that set are none other than the 1985 World Series champions (Echo: Champions-champions-champions!!!)."

"Oh wow!"

---

[20] Frank White, who is not white, always makes me think of Frank Black (a. k. a. Black Francis of the Pixies), who is not black.
[21] Thanks to my brother-in-law Paul for pointing out that Bud Black, who is not black, played for the Royals in 1985, too.

"Exactly. The judge will have to rule in our favor. He'll know— "

"Could be a she," Becki interjected. "We're not racists, but we also don't want the judge to think we're sexists either, right?"

"Okay, okay," I said begrudgingly. "*She'll* know that nobody with African-Americans in their baseball card collection could ever have anything to do with the deaths of Michael Jackson, Gary Coleman, Clarence Clemons, or Rodney King!"

"Possible objection. What if the judge realizes you could have bought that 1986 Topps set recently? You can buy those sets online, you know. How is this any different than your Stevie Wonder records, Chad?"

"Well, for starters, I didn't buy that set recently," I said. "I got it for Christmas in 1989. My parents, my sister, and more than a few of my childhood friends who collected baseball cards could corroborate this fact. Objection overruled."

"Okay, but there's something you're overlooking," the make-believe version of Becki in my brain said. "What if the judge asks you if you have any African-American friends, Chad? Wouldn't the answer to that question matter more than anything you could tell him about your record collection or your baseball cards?"

"Honey, that would be totally irrelevant," I said. "Think about it. You have to fight magical thinking with magical thinking. When you're being prosecuted in association with the deaths of African-American celebrities you didn't know personally, you have to defend yourself by demonstrating that you have a positive relationship with living African-American celebrities you don't know personally—hence Stevie Wonder and the Royals."

"I suppose that makes sense from a certain... *deranged* perspective," she replied, before a tornado of thoughts about groceries, laundry, and writing tore through my brain, whisking her away for the moment.

A few weeks after our exchange at Hastings, Becki called me on the phone from work to tell me she had changed her mind.

"You know that piece you wanted to write about the African-American celebrity deaths that have coincided with our marital milestones?" she said.

"Yes, and you sound like you're trying to talk the way I write," I said.

"Well . . . if you want to write it, you can."

"Really?" I said.

"Yes, really," she said. "I think we owe it to African-American celebrities everywhere to warn them about our anniversary. Especially those people who might be considered royalty."

"Why? Because Michael Jackson was the King of Pop and Rodney King's last *name* was 'King'? What about Gary Coleman and Clarence Clemons though?"

"If you really think about it, everyone who has died so far has been a king in some way. I mean, you said it yourself: You thought of Gary Coleman as a real-life Peter Pan, and Peter Pan was kind of the king of the Lost Boys in Neverland, wasn't he?"

"I suppose so, yes."

"And Clarence Clemons was the king of saxophone players."

"Do you even know the names of any other saxophone players?" I asked, laughing. "He did play with Bruce Springsteen, so I'll give you this one. All hail King Clarence!"

"Whatever, Chad. I'm trying to make a point here: We need to warn people who are just like Michael Jackson, Gary Coleman, Clarence Clemons, and Rodney King. Don King, for one."

"B. B. King."

"Right. Queen Latifah?"

"Ooh, good one. And Prince! Don't forget Prince!"

"Right. And as long as you overemphasize the fact that we're not racists, I'm fine with you writing the piece. Make up dialog if you need to—I really don't care. Write what you want, and I'll stand by your words. Just make sure you have a really explicit statement about how much we like African-Americans somewhere in there. We really don't want to come across the wrong way. So be sure to say something like, 'We really like African-Americans,' or something like that."

In closing, we really like African-Americans, or something like that.

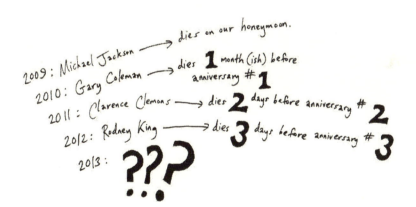

"Clarence Clemons, Saxophone King," watercolor by BARRR.

"Rodney King, King of Rodney," watercolor by BARRR.

When Pads with Wings Fly

★ ★ ★

There are many different kinds of pads in this world: Shoulder pads. Elbow pads. Pads with wings.

Lord only knows why some pads have wings and others do not. Probably for the same reason that some birds can fly, and others—the ostrich, for example—cannot.

Of all the pads in this world, pads with wings worry me the most. I suppose a part of me fears a flock of them will one day whisk me away like the winged monkeys that kidnapped Dorothy and Toto in *The Wizard of Oz*.[22]

The pad madness does not begin and end with pads with wings at my house though. Becki has a slight hearing impairment, which alters how she hears and speaks words to some extent. Coupled with her Wisconsin accent, words that belong to both of our vocabularies sometimes sound very different coming from her mouth.

One New Year's Eve, for example, Becki brought home leftover pad thai—an altogether different kind of pad—from Jade Garden, an Asian restaurant here in Lawrence.

"You know what I'm craving?" Becki announced later that evening. "Pad thai on crackers."

"You want what?" I asked.

"Pad thai. On crackers."

"You want me to put it . . . *on crackers?*"

---

[22] I assume pads with wings travel in flocks since they have wings and are therefore birdlike.

"Yes, like I always do."

"Pad thai. On crackers. *Like you always do?*"

"Yes! On crackers!"

"How will I get the noodles and the tofu and everything else to stay on the crackers?"

Silence.

"No. I want *pad thai* on a cracker. Pad thai, Chad. *Pad thai.*"

Silence.

Earlier in the day, Becki bought Braunschweiger at the grocery store. Some people use this liverwurst to make (prepare to connect the dots) "pâté."

Which sounds a lot like "pad thai," at least coming from her mouth.

Pâté. Pad thai. Knee pads and neckties. Pads with wings and clip-on ties. iPad. You pad. We all pad.

Words like these lead to the sorts of semantic misunderstandings that start wars. While Becki managed to spread pâté on crackers without incident that day, this exchange baked my noodle.

Now I fear walking into Jade Garden in the future and finding "Pad Thai on Crackers" on the menu. Or even more horrifying, "Pad Thai with Wings."

Pass Me a Scissors, Please

★ ★ ★

Becki believes she speaks English, but I would argue that she speaks Wisconsinese. Only people from her home state refer to scissors in singular noun form, after all.

As in "Pass me a scissors, please." Becki actually says this.

When she does, I say, "Don't you mean 'Pass me *the* scissors, please' or 'Pass me *a pair of* scissors, please'? It's a plural noun that has no singular form, Honey."

"That doesn't make any sense," she says. "It's one object, Chad." Of course, I never said it made sense.

"No one says 'I need to put on *a pants*,' Honey," I explained. "It's the same thing. You say, 'I need to put on *some* pants,' or '*a pair of* pants.'"

"Whatever," she sighs.

Other times, Becki says, "Pass me a scissor, please," which confuses me even more. Everyone knows scissor blades come in twos, like the animals on Noah's Ark.

When Becki asks me for "a scissor" then, I hand her a pair of scissors instead. I half expect her to say, "But there are *two* scissor blades here! Holy Hodag, Chad![23] What do you expect me to do with *these*?"

---

[23] For information about the Hodag, Wisconsin's famous cryptid, read Wikipedia's entry on the subject. A useless-but-entertaining factoid: When referring to this mythical creature, people outside of Wisconsin pronounce its name "HOE-dag," while Wisconsin natives pronounce its name "HOE-dayg."

Instead, she acts like I have given her exactly what she wants. Perhaps I have.

One night, while walking along Sixth Street here in Lawrence, Becki and I saw something on the sidewalk that validated her very existence. It lay in the grass—a singular scissor blade with handle attached.

It had separated from its twin, much as Becki had broken away from hers for the sake of love when she chose to move to Kansas for me. She left her frozen homeland to be with a man who could not even speak her native tongue.

That singular scissor blade called to her from the grass next to the sidewalk, outside of Ace Hardware—only a few blocks from our home.

"See, Chad?" said Becki. "A scissor."

In that moment, Kansas gave its blessing to a woman from Wisconsin. If this "scissor" had its own Facebook page, it would undoubtedly select "Single" as its relationship status.

"You're right," I replied. "A scissor." Singular noun form.

I could never say, "There's no such thing as 'a scissor'" again. The universe had proven otherwise. As for "a scissors," well—the universe has not argued in Becki's favor on this one yet, so I still needle her about that one.

I should probably mention that we found that single scissor blade a few miles west of a hair salon called "Sizzors."[24] I suspect the owners named the salon as they did in an attempt to reel in a) Lawrence's

---

[24] There is a nail salon only a few blocks away from Sizzors called "Chieu's Nails." An intentional pun, or simply the name of a Chinese nail salon? You decide.

collegiate demographic or b) people who cannot spell (i.e. Lawrence's collegiate demographic).

In the end, however, I see the salon's name as the linguistic equivalent of playing fast and loose with a pair of scissors—or in Becki's world, "a scissor," or "a scissors."

"With This Cloaking Devise (sic) I Thee Wed,"
ink illustration by **BARRR**.

With This Cloaking Device, I Thee Wed

★ ★ ★

When my friend Jennifer asked me to DJ her wedding reception in 2010, visions of dance floor dominion descended upon me in depraved waves. I immediately imagined myself playing the part of a villain in a western—wearing a ten-gallon hat, wielding a six-shooter, and firing musical bullets at the feet of wedding attendees.

"You people *will* dance to William Shatner's cover of 'Lucy in the Sky with Diamonds' iffin' you know what's good for you!" I would say, channeling Yosemite Sam.

While I did spin Shatner's salute to *Sgt. Pepper* at the reception, I found it difficult to discern the impact of Captain Kirk's painful plundering of the Beatles classic on the dancers.[25] I could not see their expressions of happiness or horror because the dancers—

Well, they were invisible. More on that later though.

Becki and I drove to St. Louis for the wedding the first weekend of June. We had been celebrating our first anniversary for a few weeks even though it was still two weeks away, so attending a wedding seemed apropos at the time.

I once lived in St. Louis, so I thought I would be able to locate our hotel with ease. When we followed the MapQuest driving directions we printed for the trip, however, we failed to find our hotel.

"Is this place outfitted with a Klingon cloaking device or something?" I asked Becki.

---

[25] Lest any readers imagine me spinning turntables like a professional DJ, I should clarify that I only spin the flywheel on my iPod Classic.

"Mmm hmm," Becki replied, acknowledging and ignoring me at the same time.

We had never been to the church where Jennifer and Allyn planned to tie the knot. According to our MapQuest directions, it was a thirty-minute drive from our hotel. We left a half hour early for our trip that day, thinking we would need the extra time to search for the church. As it turned out, however, we wasted much of that time looking for an invisible inn.

We eventually called the hotel and asked the front desk clerk for directions. MapQuest had misled us.

"I told you not to use MapQuest, Chad," Becki said. "Google Maps is way better."

I hung my head in shame as we followed the clerk's instructions. We soon found our hotel. It had been visible all along—just not to us.

After checking in, we had precious little time to change into our wedding attire, let alone drive across St. Louis in search of a church-sized needle in a city-sized haystack. In the end, we barely made it to the church in time for the ceremony.

Jennifer and I met shortly after we began attending the same church in Springfield, Missouri, in 2004. I initially overlooked her because she was silent as stone, and this meant she blended in a little too well with the church building, which was made of silent stones. As we became friends, however, I began to see her quiet countenance not as an attempt at camouflaging herself, but as evidence of an inner strength—and one that would later serve her well in ministry.

Shortly after I moved to Lawrence in 2006, Jennifer relocated to Jefferson City, Missouri, to work for the *Word & Way*—a weekly newspaper celebrating Missouri Baptist life. She met Allyn when she interviewed him for a feature story. While the two of them eventually pursued parallel paths— enrolling in the same seminary program to pursue Master of Divinity degrees—those paths ultimately converged at the altar.

I still remember hearing the elation in Jennifer's voice when she talked of Allyn in the early days of their relationship. I knew he could see her even when she cloaked herself in quietude. She would never be invisible to him.

At the beginning of the wedding, Jennifer and Allyn simultaneously read passages from two Madeleine L'Engle books—*A Wrinkle in Time* and *A Wind in the Door*. The beautiful babble that resulted sounded a lot like I imagined speaking in tongues would. In this flow of words, I heard what it sounded like for two people to become one, yet retain their distinct voices—a paradox that makes marriage a thing of mysterious beauty.

Instead of donning dress shoes for the occasion, Jennifer and Allyn wore TOMS. "With every pair you purchase," the TOMS company website reads, "TOMS will give a pair of new shoes to a child in need. One for One."[26] That Jennifer and Allyn wore shoes to benefit the less fortunate at their wedding is emblematic of their belief that even the smallest gesture of goodness has the potential to affect change on a larger scale, working as yeast in a batch of dough.

Midway through the proceedings at this Baptist church, a Jewish rabbi read an Old Testament passage in Hebrew. It reminded me of my faith's roots, and how often we who call ourselves Christians fail to acknowledge our spiritual origins.

A potluck of epic proportions followed the ceremony. Immediately after that, I was supposed to DJ. I planned to play the

---

[26] If every pair of Becki's shoes were TOMS, entire African tribes would have footwear.

aforementioned Earth-shattering Shatner song, a mashup of Beyoncé's "Single Ladies" and the theme song from *The Andy Griffith Show* (i.e. "The Fishin' Hole"), and Serge Gainsbourg's duet with Brigitte Bardot, "Bonnie and Clyde," among others.

This is what I *planned* to do.

"Where do I set up?" I asked Allyn. He pointed to the balcony above the dinner area.

Upon reaching my post, I wondered if perhaps I had strayed through some temporal wormhole and ended up in the Cretaceous Period. The church's archaic sound system reminded me of the computers that filled entire rooms in those old sci-fi films from the '50s—the kind outfitted with flickering lights, toggle switches, buttons, and tape reels. How would I ever connect my iPod to such prehistoric equipment?

I cannot recall how, but the church's sound technician somehow managed to marry analog and digital devices that day. Perhaps something of a kinship existed between the rock 'n' roll in my iPod and the sound system, which was as primitive as a rock.

"When are they going to clear out the dinner tables and chairs below so people can dance?" I asked the aforementioned sound technician.

"Well, actually . . ." he hesitated. "People are going to dance in the room across the hall."

"The room across the hall?" I asked, not quite following him.

"Yes."

"So I'll be playing the songs from up here—for a room of empty tables and chairs—while the wedding attendees dance in a different room, out of my view?"

"Yes, but you'll be able to hear the music in here."

"O-o-o-k-a-a-a-y-y-y," I said, stretching the syllables of the word like taffy. "But how will I know if everyone's gone home and I'm DJ-ing for an empty room?"

"Someone will tell you when the event's over."

Thoughts began to race in my head: *How will I know if people are dancing in the other room? How will I know if the volume's okay? How will I take requests?* My heart throbbed in my head like an 808 kick drum.

Half out of love for Jennifer and Allyn, and half determined to make the tables and chairs in the otherwise empty room below me dance, I began playing songs. First came "Frontier Psychiatrist" by the Avalanches—one of my favorite songs ever.

Then, knowing the church had a sizable African-American demographic, I spun Stevie Wonder's cover of the Beatles' "We Can Work It Out." I hoped the connection between my iPod and that Stone Age soundboard would likewise work out.

Becki went downstairs to the room across the hall to see if anyone was dancing, and returned to report that no one was. Quite the contrary, in fact. Someone with a baby told Becki we needed to turn the music down. To soften the blow of this news, Becki brought me a slice of cake.

I played Johnny Cash's cover of U2's "One," hoping to pacify that particular parent. To gauge audience response, Becki returned to the room where no one was dancing to the music no one was enjoying. In the meantime, I played a Japanese version of Sixpence None the Richer's "Kiss Me," knowing Jennifer loved the band.

When Becki returned from the scene, she said someone had turned the music down to a barely audible volume. With this revelation, I understood why people automated elevator music instead of hiring a DJ like Clint Eastwood's character in *Play Misty for Me* to provide the entertainment. There is nothing sexy about playing the musical equivalent of wallpaper.

I gave Becki control of my iPod and headed downstairs to survey the scene for myself. Jennifer and Allyn were smiling, and they were the only ones whose smiles I really needed to see.

They apologized for the evening's musical mishaps while Becki played "There She Goes" by the La's. I told them it was fine, and I meant it. If anything, the evening had been surreal, and we writers know that surreal experiences often make for interesting writing material.

Just as I was beginning to feel better about the evening, the music stopped playing without warning. Seconds later, Becki appeared at my side to tell me that the higher-ups had shut down our elevator-music outpost.

The wedding reception ended at 7:15. The sun had not even gone down yet. For Jennifer and Allyn, however, the marital party had only just begun.

Their love for one another—like our hotel, and the dancers at the reception—was something that could not be seen. One might even say that, when they exchanged rings that day, they exchanged more than mere metal bands. Those rings doubled as cloaking devices that robed each of them not in invisibility, but in a love that could not be seen.

Two weeks later, when Becki and I celebrated our first anniversary in earnest, I came down with diarrhea thanks to a vexing virus that likewise could not be seen. Of course, I knew Becki would take my sickness seriously. Anyone who reads medical articles about diarrhea during breakfast and reprimands her husband for laughing at such a serious illness is bound to run to her husband's side when he has the runs.

My bowels betrayed me in the middle of a celebratory lunch in Kansas City at Buca di Beppo, a delightful Italian restaurant located beneath one of the streets at the Plaza.[27] Despite my decrepitude, we headed for Olathe, Kansas, after lunch to see *Toy Story 3* in 3-D in an IMAX theater. We had reserved tickets for the screening, so I resolved not to let my guts get the best of me.

Although we looked everywhere for exit signs that might lead us to I-70 and make our drive to Olathe easier, we saw none. We resorted instead to driving almost one hundred city blocks to the theater. Becki's parents gave us a GPS device the following Christmas.

Seven months after we celebrated our first anniversary, a pregnancy test confirmed the presence of a baby in Becki's womb. Like the hotel that hid from us, the invisible reception attendees who heard and refused to dance to my music, the bug that besieged my bowels on our anniversary, and those seemingly nonexistent highway exit signs, we could not see our baby—but we rejoiced in her presence all the same.

It would only be a matter of months before I would hold headphones to Becki's belly and play music for another audience I could not see.

---

[27] I like to refer to Buca di Beppo as "Baco de Boopi." When I first called the restaurant by this name, Becki laughed. Now when I refer to it in this manner, she refuses to acknowledge my silliness. Either that, or she thinks the restaurant is actually called Baco de Boopi.

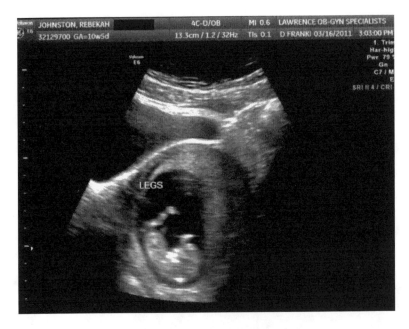

Sonogram photo of Evangeline Sofia Johnston,
taken March 6, 2011.

Blessed Are the Tentmakers

★ ★ ★

For my daughter, Evangeline Sofia.

"Can you build me a tent in the living room when you get home, Chad?" Becki made this cryptic request via Google chat.

"A tent?" I replied, laughing. "In the living room? What?!?"

When we were children, my sister Alyssa and I built temporary tents in our living room, draping sheets over strategically positioned chairs for shelter. But it had been years since I had roughed it indoors.

Becki had always nested, so it occurred to me that her request for a tent might not be so strange after all. When she craves comfort, she surrounds herself with pillows, blankets, boxes of Kleenexes, teacups filled with cherished Chinese teas, and copies of *Vogue* magazine.

She had never enlisted my help in building a nest before though. I knew male birds sometimes helped females build their nests, but—

Could she be pregnant?

We wanted a child, and we had been trying to have one, but surely it was not as easy as that.

When I was a child, before I knew anything about sex, I once overheard people talking about a couple who had been trying for years to have a child. It sounded like so much work—like mining for coal or building a railroad. We had only been trying for weeks. Surely we had not paid our dues.

Build me a tent in the living room, Chad.

The request became a command in my mind, and Becki's voice assumed the tone and timbre of the voice of God in Cecil B. DeMille's *The Ten Commandments*.[28] Being the son of a minister, things like this run through my mind periodically.

I suppose Becki's request reminded me of God commanding people to build things in the Old Testament—an ark here, an altar there. One of those building projects included a tent, too—the Mosaic tabernacle, or "tent of meeting," where the Israelites worshipped.

I built Becki's tent in the living room after work that day, using dining chairs as supports for the blanket I draped over the top as a canopy. I lined the floor with pillows, and covered them with the duvet Becki slept under before we married.

"Make it so I can watch TV from the tent," she had added in our Google chat.

Early in our dating days, we read the book of Genesis together, and attempted Exodus as well. Once we reached chapter twenty-six, however, which is essentially an instruction manual for building a tabernacle, we surrendered.

I laughed at the thought of Becki issuing similar instructions for the construction of her tent.

"Make the tent five cubits high and five cubits wide. Place the LCD TV no more than two cubits from the entrance of the tent, and on a stand made of burnished acacia wood. Place a hin of hyssop tea and seven letheks of chocolate in the tent, that I may be comforted."

---

[28] I am referring, of course, to the 1956 "talkie" version DeMille directed. He also directed a silent version in 1923.

That night, Becki entered her tent, buried herself under blankets, and watched television with our five felines. The next night, she returned to the tent again as if by instinct.

The next day—January 28th, 2011—we found out we were pregnant.

We celebrated with our friends Brandon and Joanna that night. I drank a margarita. Becki celebrated by staring at my margarita and saying things like, "I can't have one of those for nine months."

A few weeks later, Becki and I saw our daughter Evangeline Sofia perform gymnastic feats on a monitor at Lawrence Memorial Hospital. Unable to detect Evie's heartbeat with a fetal Doppler, our doctor opted to conduct a sonogram when Becki was eleven weeks pregnant.

Evie measured four centimeters long. She was a living pickle with arms and legs. I told Becki our baby reminded me of a baby gherkin.

Becki, despising baby gherkins, but not babies, decided our daughter looked more like a character from Charles M. Schulz's *Peanuts*. I have since decided she meant Evie had a bulbous Charlie Brown head, which she undoubtedly inherited from me.[29]

I look back on all of these things with wonder.

I want Evie to read about all of this someday, and know that her father took up tentmaking for her. She also needs to know that, for nine months, her mother became a living tent of sorts—a place of shelter where Evie dwelled and developed.

In remembering Becki's tent—and even the Mosaic tabernacle, for that matter—it occurs to me that we need visible reminders of the

---

[29] At Evie's ten-month checkup, we learned that her head circumference was in the ninetieth percentile for babies her age.

unseen. We need a sacramental faith—one that offers outward confirmation of our inmost hopes. In some strange way, our living room tent was a testament to the cells dividing in the dark of my wife's womb, imperceptible to either of us.

Other signs and wonders, if one might call them that, appeared that week.

Shortly before we found out Becki was pregnant, for example, we banned the cats from our bedroom, as Becki's allergies had been afflicting her. Prior to this prohibition, we never kept flowers in the house because we feared they might prove poisonous to our pea-brained brood.

Knowing we could finally keep flowers in the house, even if only in one room, I surprised Becki by purchasing purple irises. A few days after I placed them in a vase on our dresser, we learned life was flowering in Becki's womb, too.

Before I built the tent, we also watched a *Looney Tunes* cartoon titled "Apes of Wrath." In Friz Freleng's animated short, an inebriated stork delivers Bugs Bunny to a family of gorillas in place of their baby, whom the stork has misplaced in his drunken state.

I imagined Becki and me as gorillas—bumbling brutes attempting to nurture a delicate darling of our own. I hoped the stork would bring us a baby who felt at home with us.

On the day I built a tent for my wife and, unknowingly, our Charlie Brown-headed pickle baby, our cats visited Becki in her tent like so many mewling Magi. The sight of my wife in that tent, surrounded by purring worshippers, looked like a living nativity scene to me.

I treasure all these things in my heart.

"Blessed Are the Tentmakers,"
pencil, colored pencil, and watercolor by Darin M. White.

The Scatological Opportunist

★ ★ ★

"Train up a child in the way he should go. Even when he is old he will not depart from it."—Proverbs 22:6

During our first year of marriage, Becki and I babysat to prepare ourselves for the perils of parenthood. Nothing could have prepared us, however, for teaching someone else's children the meaning of the word "turd."

When we chose to screen Richard Donner's 1985 film, *Goonies*, for ten-year-old Emily and her six-year-old brother, Trevor, we thought we were standing on solid ground. It was rated PG, after all. Most of the Goonies were children, Emily and Trevor were children, and Becki and I first saw the film as children. How could we go wrong?

Midway through the film, however, a boy named Chunk calls a boy named Mouth a "turd." At this point, Emily and Trevor became quite inquisitive.

"What does turd mean, Chad?" they asked in unison.

On one hand, I was born to answer this question. I studied scatology under the "toot-elage" of Professor von Krapp at Dudu University in Fährtenblätz, so I am something of an expert on the subject.

On the other hand, I wondered if Kelly and Anne, the children's parents, would object. They had trained Emily and Trevor in the ways they should go with regard to the bathroom, so I thought they might also want to teach them appropriate language for referring to their goings. We all attended the same church, so they could confront us with ease if we corrupted their children.

My father first tickled my tympanic membrane with the word "turd" when I was five years old. While doing his duty to address the doozy of a doody in my sister Alyssa's diaper, he looked at her with fatherly affection and said, "You're just a little turd, aren't you?"

I asked him what this strange word meant. Shortly after he enlightened me, I began chanting that word as a monk might a Latin prayer.

Would Emily and Trevor love this word as much as I had? Would they become scatological opportunists like I did, seamlessly slipping bathroom banter into any conversation they could, simply because it amused them?

Of course, I knew parenthood would involve fielding questions far dicier than "What does turd mean, Chad?" Furthermore, if I did not teach Emily and Trevor the meaning of this word, someone far less qualified than me probably would. With barely concealed delight, I enlightened the children. I hoped their parents would not mind.

Becki backed my decision to educate Emily and Trevor. When we were first dating, she specialized in gastroenterology in her physician assistant work. Feces were a matter of fact for her.

"Turd?" Trevor inquired, as if this utterance were a question capable of being encapsulated in one word like "What?" or "Why?"

"You got it, Trevor," I replied. "Turd."

He repeated the word with great care, as if he were trying on a pair of sneakers for the first time. After a moment of silence, he used it in a sentence.

"I made a turd today, Chad," he said, laughing.

Emily blushed. As embarrassment gave way to a smile, it became apparent that she, too, was champing at the bit to use the word.

We returned to the film, neither encouraging the children to use this new word nor discouraging them from it. Thinking the worst of *Goonies* was behind us, we winced when one of the characters mentioned One-Eyed Willie—the pirate whose lost treasure is the movie's MacGuffin. As children, we knew the pirate had only one eye, but the double entendre eluded us completely. We could only hope it would soar with similar stealth over Emily and Trevor's heads.

If it did not, would they ask us why he was named One-Eyed Willie? Would we have no other choice but to explain that his name was a reference to the male organ? Or would we deflect the question by turning the tables on them and asking a question like, "Well, why are *your* names Emily and Trevor?"

The question never came.

Before our daughter Evie entered the picture in October 2011, our time with Emily and Trevor served as a preview of parenthood. I know I will someday teach Evie about turds, and I will probably treasure that moment even more than I delighted in imparting scatological understanding to Emily and Trevor.

In training up Evie in the way she should go, however, I am certain Becki and I will encounter questions that do not have easy answers. We will do our best to answer questions about sex, death, politics, and God, among other things, and I suspect we will feel absolutely inept as we attempt to do so.

In those moments, we will wish Evie's questions were as simple as, "Why is that pirate named One-Eyed Willie?" We can only hope and pray that we will be ready to respond to Evie's questions with candor, and that our words will be tempered with the hope we hold in Jesus Christ.

At the moment, I am thankful that Evie, who still says "tat" instead of "cat," is a long way from learning the word "turd." Becki and I have not even potty-trained her, let alone trained her in the way she should go with regard to words that might make her a potty-mouth.

One thing at a time, I suppose.

When Emily and Trevor's parents picked them up that night, we apologized for teaching their children a word they would never want to unlearn. Kelly and Anne laughed when we told them about the evening's English lesson. Anne even corrected Emily after she used the word incorrectly in a sentence.

"I turded today," Emily said, her cheeks flushing.

"It's not a verb, Emily," her mother explained. "It's a noun."

When I change Evie's diaper now, I sometimes say the same words my father said to my sister Alyssa all those years ago: "You're just a little turd, aren't you?" I know that someday she will try that word on like a new pair of shoes, and she will smile.

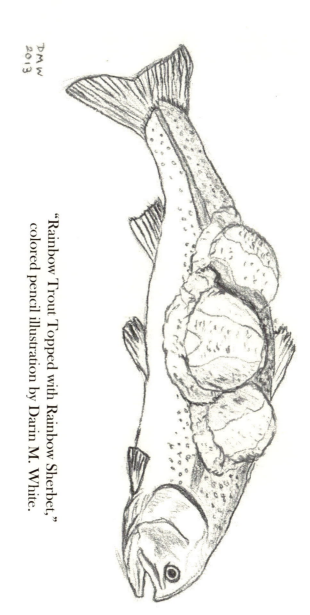

"Rainbow Trout Topped with Rainbow Sherbet," colored pencil illustration by Darin M. White.

Rainbow Trout Topped with Rainbow Sherbet

★ ★ ★

Shortly after we found out Becki was with child, I began to wonder what kinds of crazy foods she would crave. On TV, pregnant women always ask their husbands for things like pickles and ice cream, so I could only hope Becki would do likewise. My inner eighth-grade-boy hoped she would ask for even more colorful things though—like rainbow trout topped with rainbow sherbet.

But her cravings, more often than not, proved to be more confusing than colorful. One instance in particular stands out in my mind. We had just finished eating dinner when Becki began asking questions about food.

"Um, can I have some, um . . . cookies?" Becki said, her eyes wide, her expression slightly sheepish. Nothing unusual there. Becki loves cookies—always has, always will.

"What kind of cookies?" I asked.

"Oh, you know—the no-bake peanut butter kind," she replied. "Um, like those little peanut butter squares that are topped with a layer of chocolate frosting." Becki had never asked for those before.

"Does anybody really consider those cookies? And do stores even sell them, Honey?"

"Um, I don't know," she said.

Becki says "um" excessively and bats her eyelashes bashfully when she knows it will increase her chances of getting something she wants, like no-bake peanut butter squares with chocolate frosting.

"Well, we can certainly look for them," I said. "If the store doesn't have them, will brownies or ice cream suffice?"

"Um, cookies?" she said—both a question and a statement.

"Okay," I said. "Let's go get you some no-bake peanut butter squares with chocolate frosting that aren't *really* cookies."

"Actually, hmm . . ."

"What—you want something else?" *Pickles and ice cream. Say pickles and ice cream, Becki.*

"Can I have, um . . . maybe . . . chicken?"

"Chicken?" I asked. "Honey, we just had dinner. You're really hungry for chicken?"

How had Becki leapfrogged from no-bake peanut butter squares with chocolate frosting to chicken? What linked these two foods in her mind? Both were edible, of course. But beyond that . . .

"Um, chicken?" she said—once again, a question and a statement.

"Okay, so you want chicken."

"Or cookies," she added.

"So we're back to cookies again?"

"Only if there's no chicken."

"How about we go to the store together, and you can just pick something that sounds good to you?" I asked.

"M-m-m-m-m, okay," she replied.

When I imagined the chicken I thought Becki wanted, I pictured one of those rotisserie chickens—the kind that wait under heated lamps for pregnant women to pick their carcasses clean. I had never eaten one myself, but I understood the appeal of those golden-brown birds.

We walked into the store, past the rotisserie chickens, and toward the refrigerator case in the produce aisle, which houses things like butter, cheese, sour cream, and yogurt. Becki reached in and retrieved a roll of cookie dough, cradling it as a mother might her newborn babe.

"What about the, uh, chicken?" I said.

"Hang on a minute," she replied, placing the cookie dough back in the refrigerator case. "Cookie dough sounds good, but I don't want to bake anything."

She headed for the cookie aisle and grabbed a box of Pim's Raspberry European Biscuits. She pursed her lips and shifted them to one side of her face—a telltale look of uncertainty.

With the cylindrical box of Pim's biscuits in one hand, she made a beeline for the freezer aisles. She had ice cream on her mind. A big dollop of it, no doubt. With her free hand, she opened the freezer case and grabbed a carton of mint chocolate chip.

On her way to the bakery aisle, where she would find no-bake peanut butter squares with chocolate frosting if the store sold them, she slid the box of Pim's biscuits onto a shelf loaded with bags of budget corn chips.

This is something Becki does when she shops. When she decides she no longer wants something she has been carrying for a while, she puts the rejected item on the nearest shelf without any regard for whether it belongs there or not, and walks away.

"It ensures that college students have jobs, Chad," she says when I object to this behavior. "Somebody has to return (insert name of item here) to where it belongs, right? I'm keeping that person employed. I'm boosting the economy."

Becki picked up a plastic clamshell filled with puffy, powdery iced cookies topped with sprinkles. She wrinkled her nose and returned it to the shelf. Becki regards sprinkles with contempt, as though they might be flecks of Satan's dandruff.

After she had second thoughts about the ice cream, I asked her to return it to the freezer case before she could sit it on the shelf alongside the abandoned box of Pim's biscuits. She complied, but not without giving me a dirty look first.

After an eternity elapsed, Becki carried two items to the checkout lane. She walked out of the store that day with shopping bags filled not with cookies or chicken, but with Harvest Cheddar Sun Chips and a bag of cheddar cheese cubes.

To this day, I have no idea why Becki chose those things. I only know that, a year and a half later, our daughter says the word "cheese" more than almost any other word.

When she asks for a slice, sometimes she eats it. Other times, she drops it on the kitchen floor, which is already littered with debris from her dining misadventures. When she does this, I realize she is her mother's daughter—changing her mind every whipstitch, and refusing to put things where they belong when she no longer wants them.

As I reflect back on all this, I think of what Becki and I craved most during her pregnancy: a daughter. We wanted this little girl, who would have no bladder or bowel control whatsoever; this girl, who could not wear socks or shoes for longer than nine nanoseconds; this girl, who insists on decorating the floor with food at every meal.

Perhaps in longing for such a curious creature, our hearts desired something far more bizarre than any foods a pregnant woman could ever crave.

"Pregnancy Brain: Memory-Bank Robber,"
digital art by Mark Montgomery.

Pregnancy Brain: Memory-Bank Robber

★ ★ ★

Early in Becki's pregnancy, I began to think of baby Evie as a bandit bent on robbing her mother's memory banks. I imagined my daughter executing an elaborate heist in Becki's hippocampus, and emptying her brain's vaults of valuable information.

By the second trimester, I understood that the relationship between Evie's development and the decline of her mother's mind was an inversely proportional one. The bigger Becki's belly became, the less she remembered.

"Are you okay, Honey?" I asked Becki one day. "Are you sleeping okay? You've been really forgetful lately—even more than usual, I mean."

"It's called 'pregnancy brain,'" she said. "Pregnant women forget things. Ask anyone who's ever been with child, Chad."

When I asked women at church about this phenomenon, they said things like, "Pregnancy brain is real, all right. It never goes away either. Hey—help me out here. Which one of those guys over there is my husband?"

I learned about "swamp mouth" around the same time Becki told me about pregnancy brain. Swamp mouth sounded like the name of a metal band, or an affliction affecting only Cajuns and other wetland-dwelling people groups.

"This toothpaste just tastes *terrible*, don't you think?" Becki asked one night as we brushed our teeth before bed.

"Uh—tastes minty to me, Hon," I muttered through a mouthful of toothpaste foam.

"It tastes like old bicycle tires to me," she said.

"Why?" I asked.

"It's called 'swamp mouth,'" she said. "When you're pregnant, some things that normally taste fine taste like old bicycle tires or rusty tools or worse."

My inner eighth-grade boy found this delightfully disgusting. I wanted to have swamp mouth, too.

I wanted to brush my teeth with old-bicycle-tire toothpaste.

Pregnancy brain, on the other hand, sounded more debilitating than disgusting. One night in particular stands out in my memory when I think of the way my wife's brain changed during her first trimester.

In those days, her body was so exhausted from building a baby that she often headed for bed as early as 7:00 p.m. I refused to surrender to the Sandman at such an early hour. Becki preferred to fall asleep in my company, however, so she sometimes asked me to sit next to her on the bed as she surrendered to sleep.

"Thanks for hanging out with me while I drift off, Chaddy," she said to me on one such night. "Do you think maybe we could we play *Twenty Questions*?"

"You want to play a game?" I replied, stupefied. "I thought you wanted to go to sleep."

"I do. Playing *Twenty Questions* will help me fall asleep."

Becki loves playing games. Board games, card games, video games—you name the game, she probably loves playing it. Even though I seldom play games, I agreed to a few rounds of *Twenty Questions* that night, knowing it would make Becki happy.

On that particular occasion, Becki decided the subject of the game should be films. This gave me an unfair advantage, of course, given my obsessive love of the silver screen.

"Okay, I'm thinking of a movie," she said.

"Is it a horror film?" I said. I like horror films.

Instead of following the rules of the game and replying with a simple "Yes" or "No," Becki said, "No, it's a cartoon—and there's a sword, only no one can use it because it's stuck in a stone, and . . ."

"Gee, I guess that rules out *Schindler's List*," I replied. "Could it be *The Sword in the Stone*?"

"Ooh—you got it!"

This is how Becki plays *Twenty Questions*. Her version could easily be called *Two Questions*.

It became apparent that pregnancy brain was at work, however, when it came time for Becki to ask me twenty questions. I insisted on playing the game the correct way, and she could hardly stand it.

"Is it a cartoon?" she said.

"Yes."

"And?"

"And what?"

"Well, does it have any singing candlesticks in it? Or maybe a teapot named Mrs. Potts? Or maybe there's a magic lamp and a flying carpet and Robin Williams is a genie?" I am pretty much quoting her verbatim here.

"Only 'yes' or 'no' questions, please."

"What do you mean?"

"Ask a 'yes' or 'no' question. That's how you're supposed to play *Twenty Questions*."

"Well, I don't like that."

"Just ask a 'yes' or 'no' question, like 'Did Disney make it?'"

"Did Disney make it?"

"Yes."

"And?"

"There is no 'and,' Honey. Again, only 'yes' or 'no' questions are allowed in *Twenty Questions*."

"But I don't know what movie you're thinking of, Chad!"

"If you ask enough questions, you'll eventually figure out the answer. That's how the game works. Try it, Hon. I *know* you can do it."

"C'mon—tell me something about the movie. Play the game like I do."

"But that's not *Twenty Questions*."

"I don't care. Tell me something about the movie."

"But you'll guess what it is."

"Exactly!"

"Okay, fine. I'll play it your way. The movie I'm thinking of has a lion in it. So it's a Disney movie—a cartoon, if you recall—with a lion in it. With multiple lions in it, actually. Could I make it any more obvious?"

"It has a lion in it?"

"Yes, it has a lion in it."

"I feel like you're just leading me in circles. First, you say it's a Disney cartoon with a lion in it, and when I ask you about it, you just repeat what I've said. You're no help at all."

"I am leading you in a circle, yes. But not just *any* circle."

"What do you mean?"

"I'm talking about 'The Circle of Life,' Honey."

"The circle of life?"

"It's a song from the movie."

"There's singing in the movie?"

"Yes."

"Can you just give me a clue? I really have *no* idea what movie you're thinking of, Chad."

"Honey, what kind of person wears a crown?"

"A crown? What kind of person wears a—ooh, I know what it is! The movie you're thinking of is *The Lion Crown!* It's *The Lion Crown!*"

Pregnancy brain—memory-bank robber. It had hit Becki's brain hard. I imagined her remaining memories rolling around in her hippocampus like spare change.

"I'm sorry, but that's *not* the answer I'm looking for," I said.

"What do you mean? It's *The Lion Crown!*"

"Nope. I'm afraid not."

"For real? W-u-h-h-h-h—well, what is it then?"

"It's not *The Lion Crown*, but you were close. It's *The Lion King*."

"Oh, I remember that movie!"

Me too, Honey, I thought. *I remember that movie, too.*

Later that night, I threw another easy, underhanded slow pitch for my poor wife, whose brain was hemorrhaging memories. I knew she loved 2007's *Alvin and the Chipmunks*, but only because she adored Theodore. I took comfort in the knowledge that, like me, she thought the movie as a whole sucked harder than a compromised airlock on a ship in outer space in a science-fiction film.

"Is it a cartoon?" she asked.

"Well, kind of," I replied. "It's a mix of live action and animation, and it's got woodland creatures in it that sing popular songs in high-pitched voices."

"Oh, I think I know what it is!"

"Okay, well what is it?"

"Is it *The Three Little Chipmunks*, Chaddy?"[30]

Yes, Honey, and the Big Bad Wolf huffed and puffed and blew their recording studio down, and stole all their gold and platinum records. Just like this baby is stealing all of your memories.

---

[30] I would later learn that the Chipmunks were initially known as The Three Chipmunks. Of course, neither Becki nor I had any knowledge of this.

Our Hearts Are Open, but Our Doors Are Locked

★ ★ ★

"Pull a pregnant woman's leg and she will kick you in the face."–
Proposed Proverb by CTJ

On August 20, 2011—the day of Evie's baby shower—a man carrying an ax climbed out of a compact car in our driveway and headed for our front porch. Instead of calling the cops upon seeing him, however, we welcomed the arrival of this ax-wielder with applause.

Only a drama like the one that unfolded that day could end with such a deranged dénouement.

It all began with a frenzied phone call from Becki's twin at around 8:00 a.m. Katie and her husband Matt had arrived in Lawrence the night before and opted to lodge in a hotel a few miles from our house.

"What do you mean the power's out?" I heard Becki say. "How can we have a baby shower without electricity?"

Katie had volunteered to coordinate the shower—no small task considering she lives over six hundred miles away from us. With her propensity for pomp, I expected the event to be a production on par with William Wyler's *Ben Hur*. With the power out at the home of the woman who planned to host the event, I could only hope that Katie's epic plans included a backup location for the shower.

"The day's just starting and I'm already feeling stressed, Chad," Becki said after the phone call ended. "I wonder what's going to go wrong next."

Springing stressful news on a woman who is seven-and-a-half-months pregnant is never a good idea. It may be a far better idea—and probably one with a lower body count in the end—to welcome a man carrying an ax onto one's property.

"I'm sure everything will be just fine," I said. "Take a few deep breaths and trust Katie to come through for you."

I figured the shower could go as planned with or without electricity. When I hear the words "shower" and "electricity" in the same sentence, after all, I think of electrocution. A baby shower without electricity sounded safer to me—and more sensitive to Evie's situation, too. I mean, if she could develop in darkness for nine months, surely the shower attendees could endure a few hours without power in her honor.

Then again, Becki might have stashed a miniature floor lamp away in her uterus so Evie could read the fetal edition of *Vogue* magazine if she so chose. With my wife, anything is possible.

As the time of the shower drew near that day, our house grew increasingly pregnant with company—another source of stress, even though that company consisted of friends and family.

My parents had been staying with us for a week at that point, both vacationing in Lawrence and doing their best to assist their daughter-in-law in her delicate state. Katie and her husband Matt arrived later that morning, and Becki's brother Jon and his wife Jessie followed shortly thereafter.

Before Katie even said hello to her twin, she informed Becki that the power company had restored service to the house where the shower would be held. All our fretting had been for naught, or so we thought.

Realizing the shower attendees planned to meet at our house to carpool to the event, the men in the house decided to escape the inevitable estrogen explosion that would result from this female influx.

For Operation Estrogen Escape (OEE), we drove to Half Price Books and Hastings in search of musical diamonds in the clearance-bin rough. I bought His Name is Alive's *Stars on ESP* album for a dollar. None of us had ESP though, as the events that followed surprised us all.

When Katie called to sound the alarm for the second time that day, we were sitting in a broken down booth at Papa Keno's on Mass Street. Matt answered his phone while Dad, Jon, and I continued to grease our gullets with pizza.

"The girls locked themselves out of your house, Chad," Matt said.

Dad and Jon smiled at this news until I said, "I think that means we're locked out of the house, too."

Becki and I had keys for the dead bolt lock on our front door, but not for the doorknob lock. Our realtor never provided us with keys for it, so we always refrained from locking it.

Becki's friend Jen had no knowledge of this, and turned the lock on the doorknob as the ladies left the house. When she closed the door behind her, she turned dominion of the house over to our cats.

We would have been able to enter the house through the garage, but Dad had driven the getaway car for OEE. My car and my garage door opener with it sat in the garage, untouchable. Becki had hitchhiked to the shower with someone else, too, so she was in the same predicament as me.

On our way back to the house, the members of OEE decided to break into the house while the women broke into tears at the shower every time Becki opened a present for Evie.

"Oh, that onesie is *so* cute!" I imagined them gushing—their tears making the celebration seem more like an actual shower. "I could just die—it's *that* cute!"

Upon reaching the house, we made our way to the backyard. I knew the rear of our house featured five potential access points—two doors and three ground-level windows, to be precise.

In our house, we have a sliding glass door in our kitchen that leads to a screened-in porch that overlooks the backyard. To reach that door from outside, we first needed to break into our screened-in porch, which was locked.

I cut a hole in the mesh netting on the door with one of my keys, hoping to reach through it and lift the hook-and-eye latch on the other side of the door. Consider for a moment the irony involved in a man using keys to break into his own house when he is locked out!

We succeeded in opening the door to the screened-in porch, but once we entered, none of my keys fit the lock on the sliding door. So Becki and I lacked keys to not one, but *two* doors on our house.

Door number two overlooks the backyard from a deck attached to the bathroom off of our master bedroom, which is every bit as strange as it sounds. We never use this deck because our backyard is more of a source of embarrassment than enjoyment. Compared to the overgrowth of greenery in our yard, which includes plenty of poison ivy, the Amazon rainforest looks like an underachieving ecosystem.

Many things have disappeared into the mighty maw of our untamed beast of a backyard—a birdfeeder, a bird bath, and an old bench, among other things. All of these things are remnants of a once-upon-a-time backyard garden paradise—the work of people who lived in our house long before us.[31]

As we contemplated how we might reach the door leading to the master bathroom, Matt discovered a partially digested wooden ladder in the overgrowth. He managed to climb it without breaking any of its rotten rungs. As soon as he reached door number two, however, he found that none of my keys unlocked the door.

We were missing keys to *three* doors on our house. How had Becki and I managed to avoid locking ourselves out for so long?

Before resorting to breaking windows on the back of the house, we decided to direct our attention to the front door. We tried to free the doorknob from the front door with a brick from under our porch, but to no avail.

Around this time, Matt called Becki and told her that a locksmith had agreed to open the front door for us for a fee of one thousand dollars. This was a complete fabrication, of course, but it seemed like a fitting and funny thing to do, considering what the ladies had done to us that day.

"A thousand dollars?!?" Becki stammered.

"Yep—it's a Saturday, you know. Locksmiths charge extra on the weekend," Matt said.

I forgot this even happened, but Becki remembered it clearly—probably because we never let her in on the joke. We simply hung up the phone and let the gravity of the situation weigh on the women for the remainder of the afternoon. While we wanted

---

[31] My friend Tim, a landscape architect by trade, said the people who designed our backyard probably had the Hanging Gardens of Babylon in mind. Like Babylon before it, however, our backyard had fallen into decline.

revenge, I think we also believed Becki knew we were pulling her leg.

There should really be a proverb that says, "Pull a pregnant woman's leg and she will kick you in the face." A saying like that could have saved me some trouble that day—but more on that later.

After our prank phone call, we contacted a locksmith for an estimate, but ultimately decided it would be less expensive and more entertaining to call my friend Brandon, the Human Swiss Army Knife. Moments later, he pulled into our driveway in his gray Ford Focus and emerged from it with a pry-bar in one hand and an ax in the other.

Everyone rejoiced at the sight of Brandon brandishing that ax even though we never used it. We never needed to, as it turned out.

Seconds after Brandon arrived, my dad dislodged the doorknob with the pry-bar. Ministers use scriptures as tools to open people's hearts to God, so opening a locked door with a pry-bar probably felt like a trick of the clerical trade to him. I took pride in the fact that my dad, the Baptist minister, could burgle with the best of them.

Shortly after we celebrated our victory over the front door, we carpooled to Ace Hardware to purchase a new doorknob and deadbolt lock kit, complete with keys for both locks in the set. After we installed it, Becki and I would only need keys to two doors on the house.

When Becki came home, she saw that we had succeeded in breaking into the house. She sighed with relief, resting her hand over her heart as if she had just been spared a heart attack.

"Oh, I'm so glad we won't have to pay a locksmith a thousand dollars," she said. "I know we've been saving up money for Evie's birth, but we don't have much to spare."

"There was never anything to worry about," I said. "The whole thing was a joke. We were just mad at you ladies for locking us out of the house and wanted you to feel the way *we* felt!"

At that point, Becki made me feel the way she felt. As she barked at me, I could only think of the whereabouts of Brandon's ax, and hope it was not within my wife's reach.

Becki looks back on all this with fondness now, or at least with a decrease in her desire to decapitate her dimwitted husband. She would give birth to Evie six weeks after this incident.

If we locked ourselves out of the house in our rush to reach the hospital in time for Evie's birth, all would be well. Our baby would lack nothing because our hearts would be open even if our doors were locked.[32]

---

[32] Fast-forward ten months to June of 2012. After being bitten on the knee by a brown recluse, I took it upon myself to spray around the perimeter of our house with spider spray, and set up numerous glue traps throughout the house to capture unsuspecting arachnids. I even sprayed the deck off of our master bedroom bathroom.

After being locked out of the house less than a year before, and having an entire year to change the locks on our other doors, I found myself locked out again.

Instead of hurling my body over the railing of the deck and landing on the air conditioning unit one floor below, I called my neighbors Malcolm and Joyce. They were kind enough to retrieve me from my roost with a ladder.

We still have no key to that door though. I am afraid that if we change the lock, we will run out of stories to tell people.

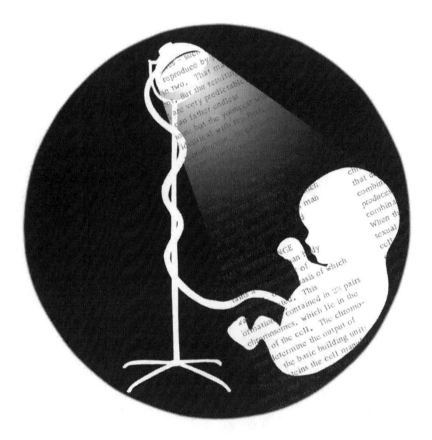

"Umbilical Floor Lamp," art by Danny Joe Gibson.

The Paralytic Shopping Spree

* * *

I am perfecting a new dance I call The Paralytic Shopping Spree. While this name is clunky at best, I suppose it sounds no worse than The Mashed Potato, The Hokey Pokey, or The Watusi.

I would come up with something cleverer if I could, but I cannot. Parenthood has zapped the crap out or whatever hemisphere or lobe or structure in my brain I have always counted on for my creativity.

Which means Evie should probably be glad her mother and I named her before she entered the world. As it is, we began calling her "Meatball" shortly after she was born because she reminded us of one. She was plump, round, and sat wherever we put her like a meatball on a plate, just waiting for her adoring parents to gobble her up.

If not for our love of the name Evangeline, the sleep-deprived stupor of parenthood might have prevailed, leading us to request a birth certificate from the State of Kansas for one "Meatball Johnston." So Evie should be glad I am only assigning awkward names to dances.

On that note, I wish to return to that awkwardly named dance—the Paralytic Shopping Spree. I suppose I should explain the origins of the name.

When I was a boy, my parents sometimes took my sister Alyssa and I to a toy store called Children's Palace. It looked like a castle, complete with turrets. If I came across such a place now and had to name it in my present mental state, I might be inclined to call it Happy Fun Toy Castle Place.

As a child, I frequently fantasized about winning a shopping spree at Children's Palace. I dreamed of emptying the store's shelves into so many shopping carts, leaving only the hot pink Barbie aisle intact. The idea of winning a shopping spree appealed to that part of me that longed to fill his bedroom from floor to ceiling with toys.

As an adult, I fantasize about filling the day from dawn to dusk with movies, music, books, and even the freedom to rapture in the sweetness of doing nothing. The only problem is, when I happen upon this sort of freedom without forewarning, I suddenly want to do everything I possibly can, which means I end up doing absolutely nothing—and not in the rapturous, sweet sense.

At times like these, I feel like I have won a shopping spree—a chance to fill my life's cart to overflowing. But the possibilities overwhelm me, leaving me paralyzed.

I sit down. I stand up. I turn on a movie. I turn it off. I put on my shoes and grab my car keys, intent on driving somewhere to buy something. I drive nowhere and buy nothing. I take off my shoes. I sit down.

So goes the Paralytic Shopping Spree.

I first perform this dizzy dance only a matter of weeks after becoming a father. Becki decides to treat herself to an evening out with her girlfriends, and she offers to take Evie with her so I can enjoy some time to myself.

"You have an hour to do anything you want," she says. "After that, Evie will probably want to go to bed. So have fun!"

I can do anything I want? I think to myself upon hearing this news. I feel like the winner of a shopping spree. I think of Children's Palace—or rather, Happy Fun Toy Castle Place. The possibilities begin to flood my mind.

I could watch a movie—or, well, two-thirds of a movie.

I could go to the record stores in town—Kief's or Love Garden—and search for treasures on the cheap in the clearance bins.[33]

I could read. I'm a writer, after all, and writers are supposed to read a lot, right? I should probably read.

Fifteen minutes pass. I have forty-five minutes to do something and, at this rate, it looks like I will spend those forty-five minutes deciding what to do.

I could watch half a movie.

I could read a few chapters from Eric Metaxas's book, Bonhoeffer: Pastor, Martyr, Prophet, Spy. I have been reading this book for approximately four score and seven years. It is 591 pages long including the index.

I notice one of Evie's pacifiers sitting atop the book, directly over Dietrich's mouth. In addition to invading our house, Evie has apparently established a foothold in Nazi Germany.

I read the same paragraph approximately 591 times. I may as well be reading the index. Only thirty minutes remain.

I could see a third of a movie.

I could go to Walgreen's and buy candy.

I go to Walgreen's and buy two bags of Russell Stover's pectin jellybeans because the word "pectin" appeals to me for reasons I still do not understand.

---

[33] My brother-in-law Jon, who has the Hebrew equivalent of "peanut butter" tattooed on his arm, taught me the value of searching for such musical treasures a few years ago. I sometimes raid the clearance racks at Half Price Books and walk away with eight to ten albums for $10. Good ones, too.

Pectin.

I say the word over and over in the car as I drive home, forming it with my teeth and tongue. By the time I return home from my candy crusade, only fifteen minutes remain.

The world is my oyster for fifteen minutes.

I could see thirty commercials, or half an infomercial.

I could stand up and shout "Freedom!" at the top of my voice, but this would frighten our five felines.

Maybe if I do this outside—maybe on the street corner, while waving an American flag—I will feel like I have seized the day.

I devour my jellybeans in a jiffy. As I do so, I wonder: *If beans are the musical fruit, what kind of music do jellybeans produce?*

Ten minutes remain.

I could read more.

I read more. Again, I retain none of it.

A half-hour passes, and Becki and Evie do not return. I continue to dance The Paralytic Shopping Spree. I am a marathon dancer like the people in Sidney Lumet's film, *They Shoot Horses, Don't They?*

How could I have known I would have extra time? I wonder. *Becki said she'd be gone an hour. No more, no less.*

Another hour passes, and I watch the clock as if I am watching a movie. I wish I would have watched a movie—but *what* movie?

I said the world was my oyster, but I am beginning to believe I am more of an oyster myself—senseless and stationary with the pressure of a sea of possibilities pushing down on me.

I play *The Legend of Zelda on our Nintendo Wii*—the original 8-bit game I played as a child.[34]

When Becki left and took Evie with her, I was playing *Legend of Zelda*, too. Which means when she returns with our daughter after being gone for a confounding *two-and-a-half hours*, it looks like I have been playing the game for two-and-a-half hours. I have not.

I have been floundering—like a flounder, which lives at the bottom of the sea like an oyster. Flounders are more mobile than oysters though, so I suppose I am nothing like a flounder at all.

"Where have you been?" I ask Becki. "You said you'd only be gone an hour, but you were gone two-and-a-half hours! I wish you would've told me you'd be gone that long."

Becki looks at me as if I am speaking some language other than English. If I had any sense, I would speak in Wisconsinese so she would understand me. But I am senseless—I am Oysterman.

"I could've watched a movie, but I didn't. I was just . . . *paralyzed*. I kept thinking, 'Becki said she'd be gone an hour. *What can I do in an hour?* Quick! Think of something!' But I couldn't think of *anything*!"

"Don't be mad," she says. "I only planned to be out for an hour, but Evie was good, and she was awake. Why bring her home and put her to bed if she's okay? I figured you'd like the extra time to yourself."

How could I argue with this line of reasoning?

"I'm thinking of going out with the girls again tomorrow," she continues. "I'll take Evie with me again. You sound like you need

---

[34] Read my essay about *The Legend of Zelda* at http://chadthomasjohnston.com/2012/05/my-250th-post-ctj-professes-his-love-for-zelda-in-the-baylor-lariat/.

more rest. So you can just do whatever you want in the afternoon. We'll be gone an hour or so."

As the reader might guess, I danced the Paralytic Shopping Spree again the next day. If I keep this up, I will be a regular Fred Astaire before I know it. Either that, or I will call myself Fred and stare into space. If I lose my mind, I can only hope Becki will tell me I am going to live at Happy Fun Toy Castle Place for awhile when she commits me to a mental institution.

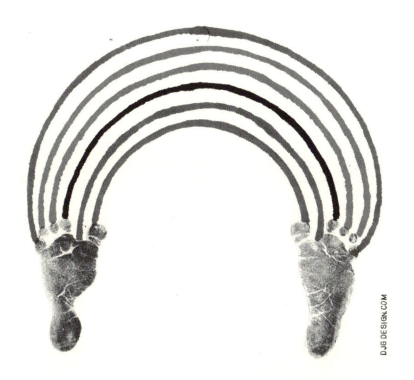

"Baby Promises to Never Flood the World with Tears,"
mixed media by Danny Joe Gibson.

Baby footprints scanned from CTJ's hospital birth records.

County Road Something-or-Other

★ ★ ★

Shortly after Evie was born, Becki and I found ourselves lost in the Kansas country at night in her Honda Civic with baby onboard. When we saw a sign reading "County Road 55240," we realized there might be as many as 55,240 roads crisscrossing the Kansas country, if not more.[35] To find our way home, we would probably need to explore more than a few of those roads—but which ones?

Our journey into that dark night began in the light, when Becki's Honda Civic died in the parking lot at Target one morning, only a week after Evie was born. The fine folks at Autozone informed us that the alternator had stopped alternating—this is what alternators do, right?

Becki's friend Jen insisted that we let her car-enthusiast husband Scott install a new one for us, as motor oil courses through his veins instead of blood.[36] We agreed to bring Becki's car to their house on the outskirts of Lawrence. And by "the outskirts of Lawrence," I mean Jen and Scott live so far from civilization that the city's Internet providers refuse to serve them.

They live off of one of those roads that has five digits in its name— "County Road 52450" or "County Road 54250," or something along

---

[35] For the reader who smells a typo upon encountering "county" and "country" in the same sentence, let the record show: County roads do exist in the country. One could feasibly refer to them as country roads, but their names—at least in Missouri and Kansas—almost always read "County Road," followed by a long number.

[36] I like to imagine Scott attempting to donate blood.

"What's your blood type, sir? O positive? Maybe B negative?"

"You 'B negative' on both guesses," Scott says to the phlebotomist. "It's 10W-40."

those lines. I can never remember the number, so from here on I will simply refer to it and all other such roads as "County Road Something-or-Other." Since these roads all look the same, the numbers do little to distinguish one from another anyway.

Using jumper cables, we charged Becki's battery sufficiently to enable us to reach Jen and Scott's house. Becki, whose radar usually rivals that of any military operation, navigated the numbered country roads with no difficulty. I sat in the backseat because we believed—however foolishly—that we might maintain a modicum of control over any baby chaos that might break out unbidden if I rode alongside Evie.

We arrived at Jen and Scott's house in the middle of the afternoon, and parked in the garage next to a stock car that had no wheels. Jen, who was six months pregnant at the time, talked babies with Becki and marveled at our Meatball while Scott and I worked on Becki's Honda in the garage. And by "Scott and I worked on Becki's Honda," I mean Scott worked on the car while I aimed the flashlight at the engine block so he could see.

By the time Scott finished installing the new alternator, night had descended upon the sleepy Kansas country like a cloud of squid ink. We thanked Jen and Scott for their kindness, bid them goodnight, and turned onto County Road Something-or-Other in hopes of going home, our alternator alternating again.

After making several turns and driving deeper into the country night, Becki said "Hmm" and wrinkled her nose.

"Why'd you say 'Hmm'?" I asked. "Should I be worried?"

"I think we might be lost, Chad."

"Wait—you *think* we might be lost, or we're *actually* lost?" I asked as we closed in on an intersecting road.

"Nope, I don't remember that road," she continued. "We're lost."

Becki never loses her way, so I had no idea what to do. I have no sense of direction to speak of, so I always rely on my wife's navigational know-how.

"Why don't you call Jen and tell her where we are?" I asked. "Maybe she can give us directions."

"I would, but I have no signal out here on my cell phone."

Around this time, Evie decided to break out into song. And by "break out into song," I mean she began to yowl like Yoko Ono on her primal *Plastic Ono Band* album.

This surprised us more than a little, as Evie had slept and suckled so silently during her first weeks in the world that we had come to think of her as a quiet baby. In our estimate, she modeled the mildness of our Lord and Savior in his infancy—at least as we imagined him thanks to songs like "Away in a Manger."

"Just wait and see," said every single soul we told about our silent child—especially those who had children of their own. "She won't be quiet forever."

"What do they know?" Becki and I said to each other. "She's our daughter—not theirs. We'll show them!"

But that night, as Becki drove down all the wrong roads, Evie showed us.

We could have mounted her on top of our car and used her as a human siren if we needed to rid the roads of traffic, so loud was her cry. Since no traffic existed on County Road Something-or-Other, this would have been a futile gesture—but we could have done it.

I plugged Evie's puckerer with a pacifier more times than I could count. Each time, she spat it out, leaving me to fumble for it in the dark.

"*Please* tell me you know where we are," I said to Becki, making no effort to disguise my dissatisfaction. The eight-pound emergency warning system in the car seat next to me continued to sound.

"But I *don't* know where we are," she replied. "I'm doing the best I can, Chad!"

I hoped we could find our way back to Lawrence. As far as I knew, everything west of Lawrence in Kansas consisted of vast expanses of crops and dust that were owned by crop dusters.

For anyone unfamiliar with the state we call home, most people who live in Lawrence tend to think of their city as an oasis in the Kansan desert. In addition to the famed KU Jayhawks, hip bands play shows in Lawrence, and we have hills, too. In a state known for its flatness, Lawrence's hills make it a geographically rebellious city.

"You know she wasn't crying at all until *you* got us lost," I said to Becki. "Why are you doing this?"

"I'm not doing it on purpose!" Becki exclaimed. "I can't help it that we're lost, Chad!"

But she had done it on purpose. I knew better. Or at least I thought I did.

At that moment, I realized how difficult it must be for parents to refrain from fighting in front of their children. A part of me knew I was only angry with Becki because Evie was crying, and I felt the need to blame my daughter's unhappiness on someone. It somehow seemed implausible at the moment that Evie would cry—flooding the interior of the car with tears—*simply because babies cry.*

Nonetheless, I learned to equate eight pounds of baby with eight pounds of pure nitroglycerine that night. Both certainly both qualify as unstable, explosive cargo—capable of changing calm into chaos.

"Chad, I have a few bars on my cell phone!" Becki shouted. "I'm going to call Jen now, so try to quiet Evie down so I can hear!"

"Try to quiet her down? What do you think I've been *doing* back here?!?"

Becki gave Jen our coordinates, and she said we should have turned left on County Road Something-or-Other instead of County Road Something-or-Other. We followed her directions and eventually saw Lawrence in the distance, glowing like a tangled up mess of Christmas lights on the horizon.

I almost cried along with Evie out of happiness at the thought that we might actually make it home that night. And by "almost cried," I mean I wept so much I almost gave the landlocked state of Kansas an ocean and a market for beachfront properties.[37]

That night, we realized we would probably fare no better than our forebears in parenthood. That we could not even succeed in keeping Evie quiet despite sitting next to her in the backseat made us feel as weak and helpless as our baby girl. If Evie ends up a well-adjusted woman, it will be by the grace of God alone.

Even more, we realized that parenthood would probably be a lot like driving on those Kansan country roads at night. We would undoubtedly spend much of our time feeling lost as we drove through the inky blackness. But in our wiser moments, perhaps we would see parenthood's 55,240 roads as 55,240 potential adventures

---

[37] I did not weep at all, actually. I only added this line because I wish Lawrence had a beach. The Kansas River is nice and all, but I want an ocean. Maybe Becki can will one into being.

and not 55,240 excuses to bicker and blame one another for our frustrations.

If those wiser moments are in short supply, Evie will grow regardless. No doubt she will flourish independent of our ineptitude.

I can only hope that she will end up with a radar as reliable as her mother's usually is. When Evie finds herself driving along life's countless roads, I hope she will relish the inseparable fear and joy that come with venturing into the unknown.

"The Keys to Her Heart," digital art by Dan Billen.

The Heart, a Home under Construction

★ ★ ★

"In my Father's house are many mansions: if it were not so, I would have told you. I go to prepare a place for you."–John 14:2 (KJV)

When Charlotte moved in with me in January of 2005, my Obsessive-Compulsive Disorder surged with such searing intensity that I had to schedule an emergency session with my therapist, Counselor Troy. I sought treatment in the first place because every time I tried to date someone, electric anxiety coursed through my central nervous system, threatening to trip all the breakers in my body.

"I don't get it, Troy," I said. "It's not like I'm dating Charlotte—*she's a cat, for crying out loud!* Why am I freaking out?!?"

One of my housemate's coworkers needed to find a home for Charlotte, and I agreed to adopt her. I always wanted a cat to call my own, so I was shocked when my body betrayed me after I took her home.

"How will I ever love this cat if I'm so anxious about her?" I asked Troy. "If all I feel is fear, how will there ever be room in my heart for affection?"

I use the phrase "room in my heart" because I have long thought of the human heart as a physical space. I asked Jesus to live in my heart when I was nine, after all, and I figured that meant my heart had to be a home of some sort.

"Do you really feel like you're incapable of loving that cat, Chad?" Troy asked. "Just because you feel that way doesn't mean it's true."

The idea that feelings are not necessarily facts—especially for someone with OCD—challenged what I thought I knew about my situation with Charlotte. Sure, my heart was filled to capacity with anxiety, and then some. But did that mean I could not add a wing to that home in my heart?

"What if you give yourself permission to keep your kitty for awhile, and just see what happens?" Troy asked.

This seemed like a reasonable idea to me. Maybe—just maybe—my anxious heart could make room for such a small creature.

I imagined a crew of construction workers toiling tirelessly in my heart to add an annex for Charlotte. In a matter of days, my heart became a cat's home.

The same sorts of obsessive thoughts and feelings that interfered with adopting Charlotte had derailed all of my dating experiences, as strange as that may sound. With time, Troy helped me understand how to transfer what I learned from my experience with Charlotte to the domain of dating.

As I made progress in therapy, more room opened up in my heart. Four months after I brought Charlotte home, I adopted a second cat and named her Sophie.[38]

When Becki and I married, she brought her three cats into my life, too. Just like that, my heart became a cattery.[39]

Eighteen months into our marriage, we decided the spare bedroom in our house should belong to a baby. During her pregnancy with

---

[38] Yes, we have a cat named Sophie, and Evie's middle name is Sofia. Judge us if you must.
[39] When Evie was born, our friend Christy made a blanket for her featuring the likenesses of all five of our felines. A picture of it appears in Appendix B as Exhibit 2.

Evie, however, Becki worried she might not have room to spare in her heart for a child.

"What if I don't love her enough?" she asked. "I want to be a good mom, but I don't know if I'm capable of being one."

While I wondered how anxiety and affection could coexist in my heart, Becki wondered if her heart was too impoverished to ever lavish Evie with love. If Becki imagined a construction crew building a place for Evie, she probably pictured them cobbling together the shoddiest of sheds in her heart's backyard.

I had seen how my own heart had expanded to accommodate Charlotte, so I told Becki I believed her heart would do the same for Evie—and regardless of whether she felt like it would or not. Becki, who has always adored Dr. Seuss's *How the Grinch Stole Christmas!*, knew the Grinch's heart grew three sizes by the end of Seuss's story. She hoped hers would enlarge for our little Cindy Lou Who, too.

During the second half of Evie's first six months out of the womb, we hired construction crews to repair the foundation in our living room. The water table beneath our property had shifted with the passage of time, causing the floor to bow up, and our ceramic tiles to crack underfoot.

The first crew jackhammered our old foundation, coating everything in our home in concrete dust, and leaving us with a dirt floor in our living room for a weekend. Our cats, which never leave our house, rolled on the bare ground, rejoicing that the outdoors had come indoors—and just for them, of course. After the workers installed new rebar and poured concrete, we scheduled an appointment with the second group of contractors, who would install our laminate flooring.

The floorers had no openings on their calendar until a month after the first crew finished its work. This meant we waited a month for them to visit and tell us that, while the floor was level by construction standards, it was not level enough for laminate installation.

We hired a third contractor to fix a few especially problematic places with a concrete grinder. As a way of thanking us for our business, he coated everything in our home with another complementary layer of concrete dust.

By the time the laminate company succeeded in installing our floor, Becki realized her heart had undergone renovations of its own, unbeknownst to her. None of the renovations involved building a shed either.

"I can't believe how much I love Evie," she said to me. "I love her more than I ever imagined I could."

We knew parenthood would bring with it a wrecking ball that would demolish certain selfish parts of our hearts whether we liked it or not—we knew it would be difficult, too. But when the dust settled after the destruction, Becki found that her heart had become a mansion with infinite rooms for Evie to enjoy.

Photo of Evie by Becki's Twin, Katie Damon.

"The Diaper Filled with Gold at the End of the Baby-Rainbow," Crayola by Baby Evie (Name Written by Amy Munsterman).

Acknowledgments

Becki and Evie, for being my family, and for supplying me with enough stories to fill a book and then some. I look forward to living through many more stories with you as we continue to build a life together, my loves!

Mom and Dad, who swore under oath that they never dropped or otherwise damaged the package the stork delivered to them thirty-four years ago. I love you dearly.

My sister Alyssa Johns, my brother-in-law Paul, and my nephew, Hudson. I wish I could put Arizona on logs and roll it all the way to Lawrence so you could be closer to us. Visit Alyssa's Etsy store at http://www.etsy.com/people/reworkedart.

Danny Joe Gibson (@DJGKCMOUSA), my brother from another mother who hails from the same mother ship I do. See Appendix E for information about Danny's art.

Jennifer Harris Dault (@jennintheattic), for steadfast friendship and editorial prowess. Visit her on the web and hire her to edit your writings at http://jenniferharrisdault.com/.

Cathy Warner, for editing skills, and for helping plug all the informational holes in three of this book's leakier essays. I am so glad I know you, and I wish everyone could read your thesis—it remains one of my favorite reads in recent memory.

Jesse S. Greever (@JesseSGreever) and the staff at eLectio Publishing (@eLectioPubs), for believing in me as a writer, for publishing this book, and for refraining from resorting to violence every time I said, "It's gonna' be another month before *Nightmarriage* is ready—I'm so sorry, man."

Brandon (@tuesdaysgreen) and Joanna Gillette (@jgillette711), for friendship, prize-winning chili, homemade pretzels, sandwiches, vinyl, and for knowing when to show up at our house with an ax. Also, a special thanks to Brandon for consultation on "My Wife, the Black Hole" and "Honeymoonwalking (to Jail)," and for supplying me with the names of three out of the four members of living African-American "royalty" Becki and I mention at the end of the essay (i.e. Don King, Queen Latifah, & Prince). I am also thankful for Brandon's work as the official reader of the audiobook version of *Nightmarriage*.

Greg Wolfe, Cathy Warner, and my peers at *IMAGE Journal*'s "Good Letters" blog at Patheos.com (http://www.patheos.com/blogs/goodletters/). You enrich my soul, inspire me to write better, and make faith seem like a sane thing in a postmodern world. Please subscribe to *IMAGE Journal* if you have not already done so (http://imagejournal.org/page/journal/).

Jason and Elyse @BARRR, and their Cheez-It-chomping children, Harmony and Charlotte. Thank you so much for the quick turnaround on the four portraits for "Honeymoonwalking (to Jail)," Jason! See Appendix E for information about Jason's art and his podcasts (which have featured interviews with Danny Joe Gibson, David Bazan [ex-Pedro the Lion], T. W. Walsh, and others).

Mark Montgomery (@markymont), for artwork for "My Wife, the Black Hole" and "Pregnancy Brain: Memory-Bank Robber." See Appendix E for information about Mark's art.

Sam Billen (@sambillen), for exotic lunches at Esquina (R. I. P.), for being a brother in constant creativity, and for generously permitting me to soundtrack the audiobook version of *Nightmarriage* with his music. Buy Sam's new album, *Places,* at Bandcamp (http://sambillen.bandcamp.com/), iTunes (https://itunes.apple.com/us/artist/sam-billen/id273968087), and Amazon (http://www.amazon.com/Sam-Billen/e/B003VRN29A).

Daniel B. Billen (@danbillion), for artwork for "The Heart, a Home Under Construction," and for graciously permitting me to use music from his "Not Alone" solo EP on the audiobook version of *Nightmarriage*. Download the EP for free from Bandcamp (http://danbillen.bandcamp.com/). See Appendix E for information about Dan's art.

Ben Chlapek (@neversleeping, @neatlyknotted), for allowing me to use "Variations on Blueberry Paper" as the official theme music for the *Nightmarriage* audiobook, and for permission to use other selections from Neatly Knotted's *Mountain of Youth* album on the recording as well. Download the album at Bandcamp (http://neatlyknotted.bandcamp.com/). See Appendix E for information about Ben's art.

Megan Frauenhoffer (@meganfrau), for artwork for "Knives and Wives." You said you were aiming for Gogo Yubari-meets-Betty Draper, and I think you nailed it! See Appendix E for information about Megan's art.

Darin M. White (@darinwhite), for artwork for "Rainbow Trout Topped with Rainbow Sherbet" and "Blessed Are the Tentmakers." See Appendix E for information about Darin's art.

Pastor Matt Sturtevant, for your support of my writing, for serving as Senior Pastor at First Baptist Church, and for supplying my family with all the sodium we will ever need in the form of your annual Kentucky Derby country ham.

Meredith Holladay (@k_meredith_s), for editorial assistance, friendship, and for bringing intellectual hipster chic to the pulpit at First Baptist Church in Lawrence, Kansas (I know I said the same thing in an essay published via *IMAGE Journal's* blog, but it still sounds cool, right?). Read her sermons and blog entries at http://windowsdown.wordpress.com/.

Caroline Langston, for early feedback on "Honeymoonwalking (to Jail)" and for writing prose that melts like butter in my brain. Also, your accent is wicked awesome. Never let anyone tell you otherwise. And when is that book of yours coming out, lady?

Peggy Rosenthal, for finding my essays funny, and for telling me so. It makes me happy that someone in the world appreciates my sense of humor!

Andi Cumbo (@andilit), for interviewing me for her "Writers Write" series, and for taking an interest in my work. Buy her book, "God's Whisper Manifesto," at Amazon.

Jennifer Luitwieler, for being my adoptive sister in scatology. Please buy her book, *Run with Me: An Accidental Runner and the Power of Poo* and follow her on Twitter (@jenluit).

Amanda Lynch, for joining the eLectio Publishing writing stable and being my literary co-conspirator, and for feedback on the first two-thirds of *Nightmarriage* (Ha!). Please buy her book, *Anabel Unraveled* (which I titled) and follow her on Twitter (@thebookprincess).

Ben Pfeiffer (@bppfeiffer), for editorial expertise, writing encouragement, and teaching me to terminate passive verbs with extreme prejudice.

Claire "Petra" Tanner (@reallifempdg), for editorial input, adoptive sisterhood, and for cheering me on as I attempted to tame this book.

Joshua Madden (@maddenjoshua), for all the press at the *Baylor Lariat*, and for the rabid fandom.

My OCD friends, all of whom make being cuckoo seem a bit cooler: Rachel, Melody, and Lindsey, hang onto your sanity, and I will do likewise!

All my beloved writing friends who are stranded on #DessertIsland on Twitter: Nancy Berk (@nancyberk), Landra Graf (@riseoftheslush), Jennifer Harris Dault, Liza Hawkins (@amusingfoodie), Amanda Lynch, Jennifer Luitwieler, Ian Makay (@ianmakay), and Jacqueline Wilson (@writrams).

Marie Wikle (@SpreadingJoy), for sending a Wheat State pizza to my wife's workplace when those first few months of parenthood threatened to steal her sanity.

Randy Townley, for patience and perseverance after pre-ordering the book two millennia before I finished it!

Mark van Dyk, for sending Evie a copy of his children's book, *Harold*. She will read your book before she ever reads mine, cousin. Buy *Harold* at http://markvandykbooks.blogspot.com/. Read Mark's ongoing graphic novel, *Circle of Blood*, at http://vandykcircleofblood.webs.com/.

Additional Thanks to: Jenée Arthur, Dr. John S. Bourhis and Dr. Charlene Berquist; "Counselor Troy" Casteel; Matt, Katie, and Eric Damon; Matt, Rebecca, Josiah, Robbie, and Kai Fillingham; Ross Gale; Malcolm and Joyce Gibson; Lindsay Haymes; Joel Heng Hartse; Tim, Rinny, and Ivy Herndon; Greg, Kalyn, Tori, and Leia Hertig; Jon, Jessie, Val Pal, and Carrie-o-Lion Hertig; Michael and Deborah Hertig; Steve, Tina, and Olivia Hertig; Jessica Hibbs-Shelley; Kelly, Anne, Emily, and Trevor Johnson; Elizabeth and Nathan Kanost; Bryan and Christy Miller; Scott, Jen, and Marin Schmidt; Dustin M. Smith; Shawn Smucker; Mark Thorne; Lorrie Wiseman; Addie Zierman; my former Allen Press coworkers; and First Baptist Church in Lawrence, Kansas—for being a family to me and my family.

Finally, thanks to you for purchasing this book. If you enjoy it, write a review on Amazon.com, tweet about it, share the book art on Pinterest (see http://pinterest.com/saintupid/nightmarriage/), and/or stand on a street corner, wearing sandwich boards that read "Buy *Nightmarriage*," or something along those lines. Also, please tell your friends about it, and tell them to tell their friends about it, unless you happen to be their only friend.

I will keep writing if you will keep reading.

APPENDIX A

140 Character Chronicles: #Marriage, #Parenthood, & #More via Twitter

★ ★ ★

Note: This collection of tweets represents a sampling, therefore does not include every tweet sent by @Saint_Upid within the range of dates featured here. Follow @Saint_Upid and @beckijohnston via Twitter to witness their "Nightmarriage" on a daily basis.

2011/07/21: Ow ow ow ow ow ow ow ow ow ow ow ow ow ow ow ow. Sound of @beckijohnston waking up with a #CharleyHorse at 3 a.m. Ah, #pregnancy. :)

2011/08/19: Forget the Trojan horse. I want to see a Trojan stick-horse. If you can hide in one of those, you can RAID MY TOWN.

2011/09/12: I am a few bearded ladies short of a circus.

2011/09/17: Hilarious: My sleep apnea test showed that I snore an average of 211 times per hour. POOR WIFE!!! Ha! :)

2011/09/21: Back from the #OB. Baby's heartbeat sounds like a horse going clippity-clop. Wife is going to give birth to #TheKentuckyDerby. :)

2011/09/21: Hilarious compliment: #OB told wife "Your urine is perfect." No one ever tells me my urine is perfect. #FeelingLeftOut Ha! :)

2011/09/22: You know you share your wife's #pregnancybrain when you reach up & press the garage-door-opener button in the car on a street where you don't live.

2011/09/23: Having #OCD and using a #CPAP machine will make me the #KingOfAcronyms, a title I welcome.

2011/09/23: Sign That I, Too, Am Pregnant: Pregnant wife sleeps with five pillows. I sleep with one myself. #iMustBeOneFifthPregnant

2011/09/23: Sign That I, Too, Am Pregnant: My bellybutton seems shallower than it did a week ago. #TooSubjective?

2011/09/24: Head Like a Bowl / Filled With Wax Fruit / I'd Rather Have / Bananas from Dole. #NineInchNavelOranges #SongParody

2011/09/26: Got to see a 3D #sonogram of Baby Evie's little face today, or at least her nose. It's a cute nose. :) Covered her face w/ her arm.

2011/09/27: Tonight's my first night with my #CPAP machine. Becki says I look like an elephant in it. I am #TheElephantMan. #HopeElephantsSleepWell

2011/10/**: Baby Evangeline Sofia arrived @ 4:23 a.m. Baby and mama are resting. Daddy is psyched. :)

2011/10/03: We're calling Baby Evie "Little Smokey" like the link sausages b/c she's ruddy & plump & she could only be sweeter if dipped in maple syrup.

2011/10/04: Our opinion of Baby Evie so far: she sucks. When she's breast-feeding, that is. ;) @beckijohnston told me to tweet this.

2011/10/06: While wearing her #StarWars onesie, Baby Evie had an inter-pants-etary blowout that looked like #Alderaan exploded in her pants.

2011/10/08: #Newsflash to Me: Every gadget in Babyland runs on gigantic, expensive batteries. #SpendingEviesCollegeFundOn-CBatteriesForHerSwing

2011/10/09: Stumpy the Raisin of Death finally fell from #BabyEvie's bellybutton! Is there a #StumpFairy who gives $$$ for stinky bits of rotting cord?

2011/10/10: My daughter is already participating in the #GreenMovement. Or at least the #GreenBowelMovement according to her diaper this a.m.

2011/10/14: The Song I Listened to Over and Over the Day Evie Was Born: #TheJayhawks' "SMiLE." :)

2011/10/18: When Evie's mad, she pumps her feet—first left, then right—like pistons in a car engine. If we break down, forget AAA. We've got her. :)

2011/10/19: I am loving my time off with wife and baby. Can I bottle these moments and pop the cork a few years down the line and imbibe? :)

2011/10/21: I've decided Baby Evie's a secret agent, judging from the unholy bombs she insists on hiding in her diapers.

2011/10/21: When Evie nurses, her head bobs back 'n forth and she closes her eyes, and @beckijohnston calls her #EvieWonder. #QuiteApropos

2011/10/21: What's in your p-a-a-a-nts, in your p-a-a-a-nts, bay-ay-bee, bay-ay-bee, bay-ay-bee-ee-ee-ee-ee-oh DOO DOO DOO DOO #CranberriesAndCradles

2011/10/23: At church, hundreds of people volunteered to be Evie's surrogate grandparents. Come feed her at night and we'll cut a deal. ;)

2011/10/24: Evie does this thing where her pacifier just trembles in her mouth like it's scared. Just kills me. So cute.

2011/10/28: Baby Evie's "Tour of Doody" has been something to behold. So many diapers for such a small baby. The kid should get a brown medal.

2011/10/30: Baby Evie is eating, like, 12 gallons of milk today. I think she's aspiring to be a really huge, tiny #Sumo wrestler. #JustCrappedHerJapants

2011/11/07: #MazzyStar "She Hangs Brightly" + Evie in Baby Swing + Othello the Big Gray Cat on Lap + Hazelnut Coffee = Monday Bliss.

2011/11/09: @DJGKCMOUSA Some of Baby Evie's diaper doodles hint at career aspirations in #Rorschach ink art, with a largely orange color scheme.

2011/11/12: Got Baby Evie in her sleepsack—her self-snuggling straitjacket—so she will be prepared for life's loony bin. :)

2011/11/14: I am happy to let Baby Evie burgle my alphabet. She can steal my R(&R) and my Z's anytime. :)

2011/11/17: My friend Brandon visited today and suggested poking a hole in the side of Evie's bottle so she could #shotgun her milk. #YIKES :)

2011/11/21: Evie sleeps with her arms straight up so she looks like a Y. She is a tiny antenna for a low-budget TV station, I suspect. :)

2011/11/26: You'd think Baby Evie would've peed in her bathtub with all that warm water, but nope. My t-shirt was a much better target. #ThanksDarling

2011/11/26: Baby Evie has #pinkeye. Poor lambchop. Going to paint my eyes pink, too, so she won't feel too self-conscious.

2011/12/03: Everyone remarks with laughter that Evie has the exact same receding hairline as her daddy. Someday she will have more hair than me. Ha! :)

2011/12/05: Baby Evie is always foaming at the mouth. She's got #BabyRabies. Hope she never bites me . . . ;)

2011/12/05: I love my wife @beckijohnston and our bundle of babyness, Evie. Their combined sweetness is enough to give sugar a run for its money. :)

2011/12/06: We have no Christmas decorations this year b/c we have no time. Thinking of putting a star on Baby Evie's head & sitting her in a corner. :)

2011/12/13: Every morning I see Evie in her bouncy chair, her limbs thrashing with delight, graceless like gushing garden hoses with no one manning them.

2011/12/14: Through her diaper. Through her sleeper. Through the blanket I wrapped around her. #BabyEvie bombs away. #SuddenBathtime

2011/12/19: #BabyEvie was brilliant as #BabyJesus in our church nativity tonight. But the children who played "sheep" resorted to fisticuffs onstage.

2011/12/20: #BabyEvie is working on a mammoth poop. I can tell. It's going to be the kind of blowout that made the dinosaurs extinct/exstinkt. :)

2011/12/26: Woke up when @beckijohnston accidentally punched me in the face about an hour ago in her sleep (I guess?). #WhoTurnedOuttheLights?

2012/01/12: I know we #Christians are the Body of Christ—each of us a different part. But it's hard to deal kindly with those who are the #armpits.

2012/01/24: Yesterday Evie cried constantly, & we went through diapers like a guerilla soldier goes through automatic rounds. #FullMetalDiaper

2012/01/25: As a child, when #LittleOrphanAnnie sang, "Bet your bottom dollar," all I heard was BOTTOM, and wondered why she was singing about hers.

2012/01/26: Choosing to be a writer is like signing up for mental constipation, for which there is no suitable laxative.

2012/01/27: A jive turkey is something the jive pilgrims served at jive Thanksgiving, unless I am mistaken.

2012/02/16: My daughter shines. Not because she's alive with the newness of life, but because she drools all over herself & the drool catches the light.

2012/02/16: With her bald head, the monk's fringe of hair in the back, and the drool, my daughter looks like Mr. Magoo with a salivary problem. #LoveHer

2012/03/01: If I eat a bean-bag chair, will I fart furniture?

2012/03/07: Clint Eastwood is welcome at our house anytime, but when our new flooring is installed this month, we'll prefer Clint Eastlaminate.

2012/03/12: If robots eat spoiled robot food, do they get #ROBOTULISM?

2012/03/12: Best Comment: Singer-Songwriter #SarahMasen (wife of @DavidDark) says I am "an ecstatic affirmer of the weird-but-beautifully-true." Ha! :)

2012/03/16: Once, @beckijohnston put alcohol ear drops in her eye, thinking they were eye drops. She screamed. I didn't mean to laugh. #SorryHoney

2012/03/16: My wife just sent me an article about child tantrums, but Evie will never throw tantrums. She might throw knives at us, but never tantrums.

2012/04/16: Worst Part of 4.5 Hour Drive Home from MO? Evie screaming, or me singing "The Little Drummer Boy" in #BobDylan voice?

2012/04/23: My wife @beckijohnston just changed her #Twitter profile: "Wife to a Twitterholic, mother to a baby who I shamelessly photograph."

2012/05/01: Caught myself humming "I've Been Working on the Railroad" just now. At work. Confound Evie's musical toys! #Curses #FoiledAgain!

2012/05/07: Oh Heaven help us. Baby Evie is crawling. 7 months into life, and she is mobile. We are doomed.

2012/05/07: My daughter won "Best Hat" at the Kentucky Derby Party we attended Saturday. But she cried when everyone cheered for her. #Hilarious

2012/05/15: I am a work in progress. Except when I am a work in regress. But I take comfort in knowing I'm always in better shape than Congress.

2012/06/02: Lost the gas cap to @beckijohnston's car while filling her car & mower gas can. Living up to my Twitter handle today. #StUpid

2012/06/02: RT @beckijohnston: @Saint_Upid you may be #StUpid but you're also a Saint too! I couldn't have picked a better husband.

2012/06/06: After Ray Bradbury is buried, I hope they'll just call him Ray Brad. The bury part will be implicit. #SaluteToSeñorSciFi

2012/06/11: At our house, @beckijohnston & I will teach baby Evie not about the Muffin Man, but about his healthier brother, the Bran-Muffin Man. #Fiber

2012/06/15: Six hundred baby wipes, two diaper doomsdays, one baby bath, some infant Advil, and a partridge in a pear tree. #TheTwelveDaysofSickmas

2012/06/24: I certainly didn't just get locked out on my master-bathroom deck & have to call my neighbors to fetch me down with a ladder. #Whistling

2012/08/06: Jesus might have had some Chinese in him. All this talk about Hui Ping and Na Xing of teeth. @Image_Journal @joelhenghartse

2012/08/22: "For the diapers / they are uh'chayyyyyyyyyyyyyyyyyyyyyyyngin."—Bob Dylan, Singing to Me and Baby Evie.

2012/08/25: Blew over the top of a plastic bottle to make music. Thrilled, Evie grabbed it & began talking into it, thinking she was mimicking me. :)

2012/08/31: Evie's been gnawing on the railing of her crib, leaving tooth marks like a beaver bent on building a dam in her nursery.

2012/09/04: Evie's first doody on my stay-at-home-daddy duty was a doozy. Man. My tweets are all scatological today! Ha! :0

2012/09/05: I am thankful for my wife, @beckijohnston, who has made it possible for me to be a stay-at-home Chad. Evie and I are having a blast. :)

2012/09/05: We got Evie a set of toy keys complete with a key fob. We already lost it. Just like a real set of keys. #MindBlown

2012-09/06: I keep sleeping poorly because I'm so excited about being a stay-at-home-Chad. @beckijohnston can't believe much happier I am though! :)

2012/09/10: "Hairway to Stephen." #ShouldaBeentheTitleofthe-FinalSmithsAlbum #StrangewaysHereWeCome #Morrissey

2012/09/11: Ooh! @aimeemann sent me two tweets this a.m. I think the rest of my hair just spontaneously fell out. #Glue?

2012/09/11: Holy Nina, Pinta & Santa Maria, Chris Columbus! Our cat Sophie just squeezed through the bars of a baby gate with only 3" bt. bars! #MindBlown

2012/09/12: "When I was a child, I spoke like a child. Now that I am a man who has a child, I speak like a child even more." #IfPaulWereaDaddy

2012/09/13: Just read "The Cat in the Hat" to Baby Evie. My first thought: What on Earth is the mother doing, leaving her children home alone?

2012/09/13: My second thought on #TheCatintheHat: How is it that a goldfish assumes a position of authority?

2012/09/17: Every time I hear the word "narthex," I think of narwhals. #ChurchgoerProblemz

2012/09/26: The plastic these baby-proofing drawer locks are made of smells like '80s #StarWars figures straight out of the package! #WeirdAndWonderful

2012/10/03: Tonight: Super secret art project involving knives, wires, raspberry salsa, Three-Buck Chuck, friends, & digital video. :) #BeAfearedKiddos

2012/10/05: I love when @beckijohnston mangles metaphors. Too cute. Today, a problem was "a thorn in (her) spine." :)

2012/10/10: I am officially a cyborg. Editing audio for #Nightmarriage on laptop. Social media frenzy on desktop PC. Smartphone in holster. #PLUGGEDin

2012/10/15: I just bought 105 lbs. of cat litter. Between that and Evie's diapers, why are people surprised I talk about poop all the time? #iAmaFreak

2012/10/18: As a child, when mom talked of "making ends meet," I thought she was talking about preparing "ends meat," as if it were a kind of roast.

2012/10/24: Forget searching for pirate treasure. Try finding the cover feature in @voguemagazine. That's far more challenging.

2012/10/25: To answer a 19-year-old question: It was probably a hippo. Hippos eat more humans than any other animal. #WhatsEatingGilbertGrape?

2012/10/31: My wife has a "Colored Only" section of her shoe cabinet. #FootwearRacism

2012/11/05: Barney is the one dinosaur that should not have escaped extinction. Seriously, explain his existence, Charles Darwin.

2012/11/05: Mom and I spent the last 15 minutes agreeing that Barney the Purple Dinosaur is not truly purple. More pink, really. #WeMightBeColorBlind

2012/11/09: Mommy and Daddy Door call Baby Door "Jambchop."

2012/11/09: Mama Pandemonium and Papa Pell-Mell call their baby "Bedlamchop."

2012/11/11: Bro-in-law Jon says "What's the internal temperature of a tauntaun? Lukewarm."

2012/11/23: The scary shovel man from #HomeAlone & the scary pigeon lady from #HomeAlone2 should marry and claim "Scary" as their last name.

2012/11/25: Each time Evie poops, I empty her cloth diaper in the toilet in front of her & say "Bye bye poopoo." Kid needs to know where it goes.

2012/12/08: Give Evie a thousand toys, and she'll ignore them and treat the nearby (clean) diaper like it's the hard-won prize from the claw machine. :)

2012/12/19: Were Dick Nixon an exercise buff, he could've been known as Richard Treadmillhouse Nixon. #WouldCouldaShouldaBeen

2012/12/28: I'm tired of hearing about the #fiscalcliff. I'd much rather hear about a fiscal cleft chin. Yeah. That would make me happy.

2012/12/28: Also better than the #fiscalcliff: a fiscal Montgomery Clift. He could help us get "From Here to Eternity" without taxing us more. :)

2012/12/31: I can hear Evie breathing on the baby monitor while she sleeps. I wonder if whales breathe through their blowholes this loud.

2013/01/05: The lip syncing of the #Titanic would have been more entertaining, no? @aaronbelz

2013/01/13: Evie understands what the baby potty is for. She dragged it out into the kitchen, said "Poopoo," and then pooped her pants. #SoClose

2013/01/14: Just because the work you dream of doing doesn't bring in an abundance of Ben Franklins doesn't mean it has no value.

2013/01/24: Evie can say "bellybutton" & she knows where hers is. Last night she got mad when I wouldn't let her show mine to our friends who came over.

2013/01/24: Evie is tearing up @beckijohnston's #Vogue magazine. Tearing those models in half only makes them thinner. #Scary

2013/02/04: Evie spilled #Kix cereal on floor. Hundreds of planetoids rolling on the carpet, hurtling through space/time like dice rolled by baby/god.

2013/02/12: Sequel to #DaysofThunder: #DaysofTundra, in which #TomCruise races stock cars on Alaskan tundra & is eaten by a Kodiak bear. @jeffholton

2013/02/12: Never let the naysayers plant seeds of self-doubt in your heart. Salt their seeds and eat them.

2013/02/12: When party poopers insist on leaving their droppings all over your creative work, let their leavings fertilize the soil in your imagination.

2013/03/11: *Delivers swift roundhouse kick to #DaylightSavings's face.*

2013/03/14: This month in writing has been 20% rapture, 30% dutiful plodding, 30% fear and trembling, and 20% rewriting the same sentence over & over.

2013/04/07: I am up at 4 a.m. with runaway writing brain. "I want to write," my brain says. "I want to sleep," my body says. You can see which one won.

2013/04/09: Evie helped me unload the dishwasher today, standing on her tiny stool to help her reach the "foffee" cups. Super cute & sweet.

2013/04/15: "The More I Clean, The Dirtier You Get," #StayAtHomeDadSlashHousehusband #MorrisseySongs

2013/04/23: Next time people come over for dinner, forget alcohol. We're serving bubble bath water. Evie drinks the stuff like a fish! #MustTasteDelish

APPENDIX B: Feline Groovy

Exhibit 1: Homemade First Anniversary Card for Becki

Exhibit 2: Cat Blanket for Baby Evie by Christy Fiola Miller

When Evie was born, our friend Christy made a blanket for her featuring the likenesses of all five of our felines. Her creation is accurate with regard to coat colors, markings, and proportions.

APPENDIX C:

Everybody's Talking but Me (I'm Yelling)

Free Virtual Vinyl MP3 Narrated by CTJ

When I was a child, I had a few 12" "story" records that both entertained and frightened me. One of those was Walt Disney's *The Haunted Mansion*. The other was a He-Man *Masters of the Universe* record, which should not have scared me at all, considering I watched the cartoon every morning. This MP3 is my attempt at creating a virtual 7" along these lines, but with an emphasis on fun rather than fear.

http://chadthomasjohnston.com/2011/07/everybody-talkin-but-me-im-yelling-a-record-by-saint_upid-33-13/

APPENDIX D

Evil: A Chili Recipe by CTJ

Ingredients

1	lb.	pork sausage, browned. Substitute turkey sausage if preferred.
1	ft.	link chorizo, browned. Substitute Melissa's brand "Soyrizo" if preferred. Note: Use the Mexican kind of chorizo that needs to be cooked, as opposed to the cured, European kind that can be eaten immediately after removing it from the package.
1	bottle	Corona Extra. Substitute Corona Light if preferred.
2		medium-sized white onions, chopped
3		cloves of garlic, minced
1	tbsp.	olive oil
1	32 oz. can	crushed tomatoes. Do not drain.
1	15 oz. can	black beans. Do not drain. Substitute low sodium version if available
1	15 oz. can	pinto beans. Do not drain. Substitute low sodium version if available.
1	15 oz. can	dark red kidney beans. Do not drain. Substitute low sodium version if available.
4	tbsp.	chili powder
2	tbsp.	cumin
¾	cup	sugar
4	tbsp.	cocoa powder
4	tbsp.	blackstrap molasses
4	tbsp.	red wine vinegar
2	tbsp.	Liquid Smoke
½	7 oz. can	chipotle peppers in adobo sauce, pureed. Hotheads may wish to use the whole can.
4-6	strips	center cut bacon, cooked and crumbled

Directions

1. Empty all canned items and beer into a Crockpot set on high heat.

2. Brown sausage and chorizo in separate pans. Using a colander, drain grease from meats before adding them to the Crockpot.

3. Sauté garlic and onions in olive oil until brown.

4. Add garlic, onions, and all remaining items to the Crockpot.

5. Allow chili to cook for two to three hours, or until taste and temperature are satisfactory.

6. Garnish with bacon crumbles.

Boom Boom Legumes: A Cowboy Beans Recipe by CTJ

Ingredients

1	lb.	pork sausage, browned. Substitute turkey sausage if preferred.
½	lb.	center cut bacon, cooked and crumbled
1		medium-sized white onions, chopped
1	15 oz. can	black beans. Do not drain. Substitute low sodium version if available
1	15 oz. can	pinto beans. Do not drain. Substitute low sodium version if available.
1	15 oz. can	dark red kidney beans. Do not drain. Substitute low sodium version if available.
1	15 oz. can	pork and beans
½	7 oz. can	chipotle peppers in adobo sauce, pureed. Hotheads may wish to use the whole can.
2/3	cup	brown sugar
2	tbsp.	honey mustard
2	tbsp.	blackstrap molasses
¼	cup	ketchup
¼	cup	BBQ sauce of your choice
1	tsp.	salt
1	tsp.	fresh cracked black pepper

Directions

1. Brown sausage in a pan. Drain off the grease.

2. Pour browned sausage, bacon, and the rest of the ingredients into a large mixing bowl and stir.

3. Pour the mixed ingredients into a large (9" x 13") casserole pan and cover with foil.

4. Bake at 350° for an hour.

Chili con Carnage: A Chili Recipe by Ax-Wielder Brandon S. Gillette

Ingredients

1	7 oz. can	chipotle peppers in adobo sauce, pureed
1	15 oz. can	diced tomatoes. Do not drain.
2	15 oz. cans	black beans. Do not drain. Substitute low sodium version if available
1		medium-sized white onion, chopped
2	tbsp.	sugar
1	tsp.	salt
1	bottle	beer (any good beer will do)
2	lbs.	ground park (not pork sausage), browned
1	jar	Original Juan's "Pain is Good" Salsa, Smokey Jalapeño flavor. If you cannot find this, use a salsa with a smoky flavor.
1	wedge	smoked Gouda cheese, grated

Directions

1. Add all ingredients to Crockpot, stirring them together afterward.

2. Cook for four hours on high setting.

3. Serve, garnishing with smoked Gouda.

APPENDIX E

About Author Chad Thomas Johnston

Author Photo by Danny Joe Gibson

Visit CTJ's Website
http://chadthomasjohnston.com

Follow CTJ on Twitter
http://twitter.com/Saint_Upid

Follow CTJ on Pinterest
http://pinterest.com/saintupid/

Follow CTJ on Instagram
http://instagram.com/chad_thomas_johnston

"Like" CTJ's Author Page on Facebook
https://www.facebook.com/pages/Chad-Thomas-Johnston/240399065994760

Visit *IMAGE Journal*'s "Good Letters" Blog at Patheos.com (CTJ is a regular contributor here.)
http://www.patheos.com/blogs/goodletters/

Read CTJ's Published, Online Writings (Archive)
http://chadthomasjohnston.com/read_saint_upids_writings/

Read Honorable Mention Essay for Belle and Sebastian's "Write about Love" Contest
http://chadthomasjohnston.com/2011/01/my-honorable-mention-essay-entry-for-belle-sebastians-write-about-love-contest/

Download CTJ's Free, 35-Song NoiseTrade.com Anthology, *Source Materials & Sorcerer Materials*
http://chadthomasjohnston.com/2012/02/download-ctjs-free-35-song-anthology-source-materials-sorcerer-materials/

NOTE: I wrote "She Loves (Like Codeine)" and "The Hiding Song/The Fourth of July" for Becki and Katie shortly after they contacted me via Facebook. For more details about these two songs, read the anthology liner notes here:
http://chadthomasjohnston.com/2012/02/download-ctjs-free-35-song-anthology-source-materials-sorcerer-materials/

Download CTJ's Free, 17-Song Christmas Collection, *Stalking Stuffers: Coal for the Stocking in Your Soul*
http://noisetrade.com/stalkingstuffers

Visit CTJ's SoundCloud Page
http://soundcloud.com/saint_upid

Note: All of CTJ's downloads on SoundCloud are free, including the 10-song Christmas LP, *All is Calm, All is Bright*, originally released in 2004.

See CTJ's Book Cover Design for Dwain Smith's *Bullheaded*
http://chadthomasjohnston.com/2011/04/ctj-creates-cover-art-for-author-dwain-smiths-new-book-bullheaded/

See CTJ's Book Cover Design for Shawn Smucker's *Building a Life Out of Words*
http://chadthomasjohnston.com/2012/02/ctj-designs-building-a-life-out-of-words-book-cover/

About Artist BARRR (Jason Barr)

Visit BARRR's Website
http://barrrheaven.com/

Email BARRR
barrrheaven@gmail.com

Follow BARRR on Twitter
https://twitter.com/BARRR

Follow BARRR on Instagram
http://web.stagram.com/n/barrrf/

"Like" BARRR's Facebook Artist Page
https://www.facebook.com/pages/Barrr/148784068490735

Subscribe to BARRR's free A. D. D. Podcast on iTunes
https://itunes.apple.com/us/podcast/icanhasjail/id393281425?i=90759362

Visit BARRR's Etsy Store & Pay for More Food for His Cheez-It-Chomping Children
http://www.etsy.com/people/BARRR?ref=pr_profile

About Artist Dan Billen

Visit Dan's Website
http://danbillen.blogspot.com/

Email Dan
danbillen@gmail.com

Follow Dan on Twitter
https://twitter.com/danbillion

Download Dan's free "Not Alone" EP from Bandcamp
http://danbillen.bandcamp.com/

Download "Sled Rides," Dan's Contribution to Christmas Compilation *A Light Goes On*
http://alightgoeson.org/?p=67

About Artist Ben Chlapek

Visit Ben's Website
http://www.neversleeping.com/

Email Ben
ben@neversleeping.com

Follow Ben on Twitter
http://twitter.com/never_sleeping

Follow Neatly Knotted—Ben's Musical Identity—on Twitter
https://twitter.com/neatlyknotted

"Like" Ben's Facebook Artist Page
https://www.facebook.com/pages/Never-Sleeping-Design/32540528198

Follow Ben on Tumblr
http://neversleepingnotes.tumblr.com/

Visit Ben's Etsy Store
http://www.etsy.com/shop/neversleeping

Download Neatly Knotted's Music
http://neatlyknotted.bandcamp.com/

About Artist Megan Frauenhoffer

Visit Megan's Website
http://www.meganfrau.com

Follow Megan on Twitter
http://twitter.com/meganfrau

"Like" Megan's Artist Page on Facebook
https://www.facebook.com/megan.frauenhoffer

Follow Megan on Tumblr
http://strangemedley.tumblr.com

Purchase Megan's Artwork
http://meganfrau.com/blog/store

Visit "Dark Potential," Megan's Virtual Gallery Exhibit Hosted by CTJ
http://chadthomasjohnston.com/2011/11/ctj-presents-dark-potential-a-virtual-gallery-by-artist-megan-frauenhoffer/

About Artist Danny Joe Gibson

Visit DJG's Website
http://cargocollective.com/dannyjoegibson

Follow DJG on Twitter
https://twitter.com/DJGKCMOUSA

"Like" DJG's Artist Page on Facebook
https://www.facebook.com/pages/Danny-Joe-Gibson-Artist/202026746482258

Purchase Prints of DJG's Work
http://society6.com/DannyJoeGibson

Visit DJG's Dribbble Page
http://dribbble.com/dannyjoegibson

Visit DJG's Flickr Page
http://www.flickr.com/photos/djgdesign/

Visit DJG's Tumblr Page
http://dannyjoegibson.tumblr.com/

Visit DJG's Delightful "Unflattering Pauses" Page
http://unflatteringpauses.tumblr.com/#about

Visit DJG's Vimeo Page
http://vimeo.com/dannyjoegibson

Gibson Goodies

DJG and CTJ appeared together on Kansas City, Missouri NPR affiliate KCUR's *Central Standard* morning show on August 31, 2011 in support of his *Quietly Contributing: Poster Art of DJG Design* exhibit, which featured over 1,000 pieces of work. The exhibit served as a comprehensive retrospective of the album art, concert posters, and other ephemera Danny created under the moniker "DJG Design." It was open to the public from September-November at the 1819 Central Event Space + Gallery in Kansas City's Crossroads Arts District.

Download the MP3 of the KCUR Broadcast Featuring DJG & CTJ Here:
http://www.podtrac.com/pts/redirect.mp3/kcurstream.umkc.edu/central/Central_8-31-2011.mp3

To promote the *Quietly Contributing* exhibit, DJG and CTJ released a free, 35-song double album titled *DJG Was Here* via NoiseTrade.com. It featured contributions from singer-songwriters and bands that benefitted from Danny's DJG Design work over the course of the past decade. Featured artists included namelessnumberheadman, the Elms, Elevator Division, Lee Bozeman (formerly of Luxury), the ACB's, Dan and Sam Billen (formerly of the Billions), as well as CTJ himself (with the song "Wrecked Ships, Crashed Planes").

Download *DJG Was Here*
http://noisetrade.com/djgwashere

Download three exclusive MP3s and view the exhibit's promotional poster, press release, digital press kit, and other related ephemera from the *Quietly Contributing* exhibit here:
http://chadthomasjohnston.com/2011/08/%E2%80%9Cquietly-contributing-%E2%80%93-poster-art-of-djg-design-free-exhibit-in-kansas-city-free-35-song-album/

Read About the Bands That Contributed to *DJG Was Here*
http://chadthomasjohnston.com/2011/08/djg-lp-a-to-z-band-bios/

To promote the *Quietly Contributing* exhibit further, Danny appeared as the featured guest on Lawrence, Kansas-based artist/personality Jason Barr's (@BARRR) *A. D. D. Podcast*. Download the seventy-minute podcast here:
http://barrrheaven.com/2011/08/d-j-g-x-a-d-d/

See the Music Videos Danny Created for the Following Songs:

David Seume's "Will Ya Be My Friend? (2010)—Danny created this video with Brooklyn-based artist Philip Cheaney.
https://www.youtube.com/watch?v=Je-O05qSFXc

David Åhlèn and Andreas Eklöf's "Det är en Ros Utsprungen" (2011, for Sam Billen's alightgoeson.org Project)
http://alightgoeson.org/?p=68

Sam Billen's "Choices" (2012)
http://sambillen.com/blog/13553231

The ACB's "The Ocean" (2012)
http://nyc.thedelimagazine.com/node/11483

About Artist Mark A. Montgomery

Visit Mark's Website
http://www.markamontgomery.com

Email Mark
mark@markamontgomery.com

Follow Mark on Twitter
https://twitter.com/MarkyMont

"Like" Mark's Illustration Page on Facebook
http://www.facebook.com/pages/Mark-A-Montgomery-Illustration/164292350269088

Purchase Mark's T-shirts and Other Goodies
http://www.zazzle.com/markamontgomery

Read Mark's Blogger Page
http://bluesaccordingtomark.blogspot.com/

"In 2012, *The Springfield News-Leader* did a feature story on some of the silly cartoons I started drawing of city leaders. It was a very nice article and serves as a biography of sorts. My illustrations and caricatures have grown even since then, but the people and inspirations that got me started will never change. Check out the full story at: http://sgfnow.co/ZWtm0e"—Mark

About Artist Darin M. White

Visit Darin's Website
http://www.darinwhite.com/

Email Darin
darin.white@gmail.com

Follow Darin on Twitter
https://twitter.com/darinwhite

"Like" Darin's Facebook Artist Page
https://www.facebook.com/DarinMWhiteArtist

Represented by Hava Studios
http://www.havastudios.com/
785.842.2216

Visit Darin's Blog
http://darinwhite.wordpress.com/

Made in the USA
Charleston, SC
18 December 2013